THE BLESSED SACRAMENT
AND THE MASS

SAINT THOMAS AQUINAS

THE
BLESSED
SACRAMENT
AND
THE MASS

Translated, with notes, by Rev. F. O'Neill

Roman Catholic Books

Post Office Box 2286, Fort Collins, CO 80522

BooksforCatholics.com

Nihil Obstat:
Hubertus Richards, S.T.L., L.S.S.
Censor Deputatus

Imprimatur:
E. Morrogh Bernard
Vic. Gen.

Westmonasterii, die 7a Maii 1955

ISBN 1-929291-69-8

CONTENTS

PREFACE

THIS little work is an attempt to put in a brief compass all that St Thomas wrote in his Theological *Summa* on the Sacrament of Love, and to make him more easily understood by those who are reading him for the first time.

But there are two difficulties: First, the Angelic Doctor took it for granted that his readers knew philosophy as he did.

And they must have known it well, when he wrote in his preface that his work was intended for beginners!

But in his day there were no newspapers, no cinemas, radios or television to distract them.

Now, when the public are almost surfeited with these, and with light reading of varying worth, it wants the gold in small quantities.

Scholastic Philosophy is such; but to the ordinary man all philosophy is associated with definitions, abstractions, and generalizations; and these bore.

And only those deeply versed in this subject can appreciate and admire: whereas a masterpiece in music or painting appeals even to the untutored.

Another difficulty is: How can the *Summa*, which from its very name should be brevity itself, become more condensed and yet more easily understood? As the poet truly sings: 'When I try to be brief I become obscure.'

This is the task the compiler had to face, and if he has succeeded ever so little, it is to Father Michael McGrath, S.J., Milltown Park, Dublin, that the reader and himself are particularly indebted.

It is a paradox to say that one who eats no idle bread can always be ready to assist: and Father Michael McGrath in the midst of intense pressure of work found time to simplify, and make clear, what was often obscure and too condensed, and the writer availed himself of his explanations particularly in the special introduction to some of the questions.

There is another, who has few equals in the domain of scholastic philosophy, to whom the compiler is also deeply indebted.

But in spite of expert advice, errors are inevitable and if the compiler be accused of distorting the *Summa*, the fault will be due to his endeavours to give, in the words of St Thomas, '*milk* to the little ones to drink and *not meat*'.

The Latin Text used by the compiler, Marietti's of Turin, 15th edition, 1925, is exactly the same even to the footnotes as Nutt's Edition published in London in 1874.[1]

Both must differ very slightly from the Leonine edition used by the English Dominicans to whose monumental work[2] this little effort owes its inspiration and which made its compilation a comparatively easy task.

---

1 This edition was probably edited by Abbé Drioux. It contains a letter from Pius IX congratulating him on the translation of the *Summa* into French.
2 *The Summa Theologica* literally translated by the English Dominican Fathers, 22 volumes, published by Burns, Oates, & Washbourne Ltd., London.

INTRODUCTION

I

TERMS USED IN PHILOSOPHY

THE object of the compiler is to give the ordinary layman an opportunity of reading in as simple a form as possible one of the noblest works ever written.

But as the subject matter deals with difficult questions in philosophy, a few words are added in parentheses, or in footnotes, to make the meaning as clear as possible to those who have never studied that science which is the handmaid of all others.

No one can equal St Thomas in clearness and simplicity, because he thoroughly understood what he was writing about; and above all *because he believed*.

But he necessarily refers in this part of his *Summa* to such terms as 'time', 'space', 'matter', 'form', 'Dimensions' and especially to 'Substance' and 'Accidents'; and what do they exactly mean?

Only those who have made a deep study of philosophy can form a clear idea. Most of us might say with St Augustine: 'If you do *not* ask me what time is, *I know*. If you *do* ask me, I *know not*.' Or we might say with Cardinal Newman, 'What do I know about substance? As much as the greatest philosopher; and that is nothing'. Still, we should have at least some faint idea of what such terms as substance and accidents *do* mean, and above all what they *do not*.

II

SUBSTANCE AND ACCIDENTS

The Ancient Mariner exclaimed in mid-ocean, 'Water, water everywhere, Nor any drop to drink.' Substances are all round us and not a single one can we see. We may detect their presence through their accidents: shape, colour, weight, size, taste, odour, coldness, heat, etc., but the substances themselves remain hidden from our material eye.

Substances can only be perceived by the eye of the mind and hence we shall hear St Thomas say that they are the proper object of the intellect (O. 75, 5 ad 2.). Substance from its very name 'standing under' denotes something stable. It is that which upholds appearances or accidents and hence must remain hidden itself, just like the foundation of a house, but with this difference: we can strip the foundation and lay it bare, but never can we perceive a substance even with the aid of the most powerful microscope.

Substance is not only invisible but it is also indivisible unless by reason of quantity (*Summa*, P.I. 50, 2).

It is not concentrated in any one point more than in another.

It is not distributed in parts. Wherever it is, it is whole and entire and always denotes something that exists of itself. Substance sustains those things called accidents which cannot exist of themselves unless by a miracle, such as the taste, odour, colour, shape, and quantity of the bread and wine which we find in the Blessed Sacrament; and hidden under these; is no longer the substance of the bread and wine, but the body and blood of Christ really, truly and substantially present independent of his own proper quantity and dimensions. That is, as he is now in heaven, or was visibly on earth.

III

QUANTITY AND DIMENSIONS

What are they? We are looking at them when reading this page. They are accidents that envelop the substance of the paper, namely, length, breadth, and thickness or dimensive quantity, which is called a primary accident; because it is the *subject* of all other accidents as we shall see later.

IV

SUBJECTS AND ACCIDENTS

But what is meant here by a subject? And what has it to do with accidents?

We generally understand by a *subject*, a person living under the protection and laws of a certain country, and by an accident an unexpected mishap.

Here, the meaning of both is very different: an accident is something that inheres in something else,[1] which is called a *subject*; and it may be a substance or another accident such as dimensive quantity.

For instance the area or dimensive quantity of this page can receive different shapes; being made of paper, it is flexible, easily torn, or easily ignited: These are all accidents inhering in the dimensive quantity (of the paper) which is the *subject* of these different qualities or other accidents.

But the substance of the paper itself is independent of them all; and so is any other substance from its own peculiar set of accidents.

1 St Thomas's definition: *cui competit esse in abo.*

V

THE REAL PRESENCE

Hence, when the substance of the bread and wine is changed into the Body and Blood of Christ, their peculiar accidents such as colour, taste, power of inebriating (in the case of wine) remain; and hidden under them is Christ himself.

Now, St Paul tells us 'There is luxury in wine'; yet when it is consecrated it becomes the 'wine springing forth virgins'; proving to us that though our Lord is hiddenness itself under the sacramental veils, still those who worthily receive him know by faith and from experience that he is there.

Indeed the Blessed Sacrament is the one and only school of purity and real refinement.

For there are millions who call themselves Christians and deem themselves cultured, and yet refuse to believe what Christ tells them when he says: '*This is my body*', '*This is my blood*'.

On the other hand, Catholics, no matter how lowly, always take Christ at his word; proving that they are the real believers and really refined; for how often might they say with St Paul when they receive their Creator at the altar: 'I live; not I; Christ lives in me.'

Chapter I

OF THE SACRAMENT OF THE EUCHARIST (QUESTION 73 SUMMA THEOLOGICA, THIRD PART)

Is the Eucharist a Sacrament? (73, 1)

YES. In the prayer in the Missal for the living and dead, it is said: 'May this sacrament not make us liable to punishment.'

The sacraments are instituted to help man's spiritual life which bears a resemblance to the life of his body.

In his bodily life, man is born, grows, and needs food: in his spiritual life he needs Baptism or spiritual re-birth, Confirmation, or spiritual growth, and the Eucharist which is spiritual food.

Objection I. But if it is a sacrament, it would be perfected by the use of matter as Baptism is by spiritual washing, and Confirmation by signing with chrism.

Reply. A thing may be sacred in two ways: absolutely and relatively.

The Eucharist is absolutely sacred since it contains Christ's Body: Baptism, Confirmation, and Extreme Unction are relatively sacred, since the sanctifying power they contain is completed only when the matter is applied to sanctify the individual: The Eucharist is completed by the consecration of the matter itself.

Is the Eucharist the greatest of all the Sacraments? (Q. 65, 3)

Yes. Dionysius says no one can arrive at hierarchical perfection unless by the most divine sacrament (*Eccl. Hierarch.* C.3.)

It is the greatest of all the sacraments for three reasons: First, because Christ himself is contained in it substantially, whilst in the other sacraments there is only a certain instrumental power derived from Christ's power. Now what is contained essentially surpasses what is present only by participation.

Secondly, because all the other sacraments are ordained to this sacrament as to their end: order is instituted for its consecration, Baptism for its reception, Penance and Extreme Unction to prepare one to receive it worthily, Confirmation to perfect man so as not to fear to abstain from receiving it.[1] Matrimony relates to this sacrament in so far as it signifies the union of Christ with the Church, of which union the Eucharist is a figure. Hence the Apostle says (Eph. 5, 32): *This is a great sacrament; but I speak of Christ and the Church.*

Thirdly, because nearly all the sacraments are consummated in the Eucharist, as is evident from the fact that those who are ordained receive Holy Communion and also those who are baptized, if adults.

Is the Eucharist one Sacrament or many? (Q. 73, 2)

It is only one. Anything is said to be one not only if indivisible or continuous but also if complete in perfection when it has all it needs for its end, as for instance a man or a house.

The whole man is made up of all the members necessary for the operations of the soul: and a complete house has all the parts required to make it habitable.

So the Eucharist is one, complete in perfection, since it is a spiritual refreshment made like to bodily refreshment, being food and drink.

---

1 For instance if anyone is conscious of having committed a mortal sin, and is afraid to abstain through human respect without previously confessing the sin: if a confessor is available, he must prove himself worthy by a good confession.

Hence our Lord says: 'My flesh is meat indeed, my blood is drink indeed' (John 6, 56). This sacrament is therefore materially many, but *formally*[1] and perfectively one.

This answer meets the three objections proposed by St Thomas, especially the last, namely: 'There is a twofold consecration therefore there is a twofold sacrament.' Materially it is twofold but in all other respects one.

Is the Eucharist necessary for Salvation? (Q. 73, 3)

Yes; but not in the same way as Baptism is.

Do not imagine, says St Augustine, that those children cannot have life who do not (actually) receive the body and blood of Christ.

In this sacrament two things are to be considered: the sacrament itself and its chief effect (*res sacramenti*)[2] which is unity of the mystical body.

Without that unity there can be no salvation; for no one is saved outside the Church—just as no one was saved outside the Ark.

Now the dominant effect of any sacrament can be had before its actual reception by the very desire of receiving it (68, 2).

Hence the wish to receive this sacrament can save— just as the desire of Baptism does (68, 2).

1 Formally here may mean 'strictly speaking' or 'essentially' as St Thomas teaches that the two Consecrations belong to the essence of the Sacrifice and necessarily by Divine Law.

  Other theologians say that only one Consecration suffices. The great commentators, à Lapide and Maldonatus, hold that our Lord consecrated the Eucharist under the one species in the house of Cleophas (cf. Luke xxiv, 30). St Jerome and St Augustine are of this opinion.

2 The expression 'res sacramenti' occurs frequently and will be translated generally by 'dominant' or 'crowning effect' or 'peculiar effect'—For instance in Baptism it is the washing away of original sin: in Confirmation spiritual strength and so forth.

But there are two differences:

First, Baptism is the beginning of spiritual life and the gate of the sacraments. The Eucharist is the consummation of that life and the end of all the sacraments. They sanctify and prepare for its reception and consecration (65, 3).

Therefore as spiritual life can only begin with Baptism so the Eucharist must perfect it—not by actual reception alone but by desire; for the end is attained in wish and intention.

Secondly, Baptism ordains man for the Eucharist (that is, Baptism makes him a fit subject for consecrating or receiving it). And just as children when baptized believe by the *faith* of the Church, so by the *intention* of the Church do they desire this sacrament.

In this way they receive the chief effect of the Eucharist. But they are not pre-ordained to Baptism by any other sacrament: therefore *before* its reception whilst adults can receive Baptism by desire, *children have not in any way that desire.* Hence they cannot receive the chief effect of Baptism without receiving the sacrament itself.[1] Therefore the Eucharist is not necessary for salvation in the way Baptism is.

Obj. I. The Eucharist should be necessary for salvation in the same way as Baptism: for our Lord said, 'Except

---

[1] These words of St Thomas give one reason why Pius V ordered Cajetan's written opinion to be expunged from his works, viz. 'Children who cannot actually be baptized may be saved by the faith of their parents manifested by some external sign—just as children were saved under the Old Law.'

But parents should certainly pray for their unborn children; for again St Thomas says of these: 'Children cannot be subject to the action of men so as to receive the sacrament unto salvation: *they can however be subject to the action of God before whom they live so that by a privilege of grace they may obtain sanctification, as is evident from those who were sanctified in the womb.*' (P. III, Q. 68, Art. XI, ad I.)

'Possunt tamen subjici operationi Dei apud quem vivunt ut quodam privilegio gratiae santificationem consequantur—sicut patet de sanctificatis in utero.'

you eat the flesh of the Son of Man and drink his blood you shall not have life in you' (John vi, 54).

Reply: No. For St Augustine says, 'Every one of the faithful becomes a partaker of the body of Christ when in Baptism he is made a member of Christ's body.

Obj. II. The Eucharist is a spiritual food. But bodily food is needed for bodily health; therefore this sacrament is needed for spiritual health.

Reply: Corporal food is changed into the substance of the person nourished and it must be taken and digested. Spiritual food changes man into itself according to Saint Augustine who heard our Lord saying, 'Thou shalt not change me into thee as food of the flesh, but thou shalt be changed into me'. But one can be changed into Christ by desire without actually receiving this sacrament: so the comparison does not hold.

Why is the Blessed Sacrament called by various names?

(Q. 73, 4)

Because it comprehends by a threefold signification, the past, the present, and the future:

The Past: For it is called a sacrifice, since it commemorates the Passion which is a true sacrifice (3. 48. 3.).

The Present: For it means ecclesiastical unity; and therefore is called Communion: 'Because', says St John Damascene, 'we partake of Christ's flesh and Godhead; and we communicate with one another through it; and by it are united.'

The Future: For it is called the Viaticum because it provides the way to eternal glory and foreshadows its enjoyment. For the same reason it is called the Eucharist, that is grace, gratitude, or surpassing beauty; because the grace of God is life everlasting (Rom. 6, 23); or because it really contains Christ, who is full of grace. The Greeks call it Metalepsis or Assumption; for St John Damascene

B

says: 'We thereby assume the Godhead of the Son'.

Obj. I When it is one sacrament it should not be called by various names.

Reply: The same thing can be called by various names according to its different effects.

Obj. II. A species is not distinguished by what is com-mon[1] to the whole genus but the Eucharist is a sacrament of the New Law; and it is common to all the sacraments to confer grace which the Eucharist means, viz., 'good grace'. Moreover all the sacraments supply us with a remedy through the journey of life which belongs to the idea of a Viaticum and something sacred is done in all the sacraments which should imply a sacrifice. Again all the faithful communicate with one another through all the sacraments which the Greek word *synaxis* and the Latin *communio* signify; therefore these names are not suitable to this Sacrament.

Reply: What is common to all is autonomastically (i.e. making the individual stand for the species) attributed to the Eucharist on account of its excellence.

Obj. III. The Eucharist is a sacrament: therefore it is not properly called a sacrifice. Neither should it be termed a host or a victim.

Reply: The Eucharist is called a sacrifice since it re-pre-sents the Passion of Christ (that is, it re-presents the same Victim with the self-same will to suffer and to die once; and produces the same effects). It is also termed a host since it contains Christ, who is a Host of Sweetness (Eph. 5, 2).

Was the Last Supper a proper time to institute this Sacrament?
(Q. 73, 5)

Yes.

---

[1] For instance I do not distinguish an oak from all other trees if I simply say: an oak has leaves and branches.

(1) For when Christ was about to leave his disciples as mortal man, he left himself present under the sacramental veils just as an emperor's image is erected to be honoured in his absence.

(2) If there is no faith in the Passion there is no salvation (cf. Rom. 3, 33). There must be something therefore to show forth the Passion: In the Old Law it was prefigured by the chief sacrifice, namely the paschal lamb: in the New, the Eucharist takes its place and commemorates what is past just as the paschal lamb was figurative of the Passion to come.[1]

(3) A third reason is: The words of parting friends are best remembered. Then affection is strongest; and what affects us most makes the deepest impression. So our Lord chose to institute this sacrament when leaving his disciples for the last time, that it might be more revered.

Obj. But a commemoration refers to things past: then this sacrament should not have been instituted before the Passion.

Reply: When our Lord instituted it at the Last Supper, he meant it to be a future memorial to his Passion *as accomplished*, according to the words of the Canon of the Mass: '*As often as you shall do these things: You shall do them in memory of me.*' Wherein the future is implied.

Was the Paschal Lamb the chief figure of this Sacrament?
(Q. 73, 6)

Yes. It foreshadowed the Eucharist in three ways:

First: The sacrament only, namely the sensible sign or appearance of bread and wine.

---

1 A reason given here from St Leo in Marietti's edition is omitted in the Dominican translation of the Leonine edition, viz.: 'That the shadows might yield to the substance; for the ancient observance is ended by the new sacrament—victim is changed to victim; blood is removed by blood; and a legal festival whilst changed is fulfilled.' (Serm. 7, De Pass. Dom. c. 1 in fin.) A single omission in a work of such vast extent is no small tribute to its accuracy and fulness.

Second: The reality—that is Christ's body.

Third: The peculiar effect.

(1) *Of the sacrament only:* the chief figure was the offering of Melchisedech—bread and wine.

(2) *Of the reality:* namely, Christ suffering, contained in this sacrament—the figures were all the sacrifices of the Old Testament especially the sacrifice of expiation, the most solemn of all.

(3) *Of its peculiar effect:* the principal figure was the manna which 'contained the sweetness of every taste' (Wisdom 16, 20), just as the grace of the sacrament refreshes the mind in every way.

The paschal lamb prefigured the Eucharist in these three ways:

(1) It was eaten with unleavened bread according to Exod. 12, 5.

(2) It was immolated on the fourteenth day of the moon, which was a figure of the Passion of Christ who was called a lamb on account of his innocence.

(3) By its effects. The Israelites were saved from the destroying angel and brought from Egyptian captivity.

Chapter II

THE MATTER OF THIS SACRAMENT

Is the matter of this Sacrament Bread and Wine? (Q. 74, 1)
YES. And for good reasons. First, as regards the use of
this sacrament which is eating.

For as water cleanses spiritually in Baptism and is used
ordinarily for bodily cleansing, so bread and wine with
which men are nourished are used in this sacrament for
spiritual eating.

Second: In the Passion, the blood was separated from
the body: in this sacrament, which is a memorial of
Calvary, the bread is received by itself as the sacrament of
the body, and the wine as the sacrament of the blood.

A third is the effect on each partaker.

St Ambrose says: 'This sacrament avails for the defence
of soul and body.'

Christ's Body is offered under the appearance of bread
for the health of the body, and under the appearance of
wine for the health of the soul—according to Lev. 17,
14, '*The life of the animal is in the blood.*'

Finally, the reasonableness is seen in the effect on the
whole Church composed of many members, just as bread
is made from many grains, and wine from many grapes.

Obj. The flesh of animals ought to be the matter of this
sacrament, just as it was of the sacraments under the Old
Law: For it shows forth Christ's Passion more fully than
bread and wine do.

Reply: The flesh of animals more vividly represents the
bloody sacrifice of Calvary; but it is less suited for the

general use of the Eucharist, or for signifying the unity of the Church.

Is a determinate quantity of Bread and Wine necessary for the matter of this Sacrament? (Q. 74, 2)

No. There is no quantity, however great or however small,[1] which cannot be consecrated.

The purpose of this sacrament is its use for the faithful. But the number of the faithful is not determinate. Therefore the quantity of the matter to be consecrated cannot be restricted.

Obj. If one is baptized in the sea, all the water is not sanctified; therefore a superfluous quantity of bread cannot be consecrated in this sacrament. Moreover a priest would only be mocking it, if he intended to consecrate all the bread in the market, and all the wine in the cellar.

Reply. There is no parallel: It is the use of the matter that perfects the sacrament of Baptism: and only what is used becomes sacramental. In the Eucharist the matter itself is consecrated. Hence, it does not appear to be true what some maintained—that a priest could not, for instance, consecrate all the bread in the market, or all the wine in a cask: because the reason for determining matter is derived from its disposition to an end, just as a saw is made of iron to adapt it for cutting.

Is Wheaten Bread required for the matter of this Sacrament? (Q. 74, 3)

Yes. For matter generally used by men is also used in the sacraments. Wheaten bread is very common and strengthening and therefore denotes the effect of the sacrament more suitably than any other.

Obj. I. Barley bread seems more appropriate to the Passion, as it is more bitter and we read in St John (Ch. 6) that Christ fed the multitude with barley loaves.

---

[1] Provided it is perceptible; for a sacrament is to be a sensible sign.

Reply. Barley typifies the harshness of the Old Law; and St Augustine says 'The pith of barley is enclosed in very tenacious fibre denoting the Law, or the people not yet free from carnal desire, which clings to their hearts as fibre does to the barley flour.' But this sacrament belongs to Christ's sweet yoke, and is suited to the truth now manifest to a spiritual people.

Obj. III. Mixing dissolves species. It is hard to get pure wheaten flour; therefore it does not seem to be proper matter for this sacrament.

Reply. Moderate mixing does not alter the species—for the little is absorbed, so to speak, by the greater. But if the mixing be notable, say of equal parts or nearly so, such mixing alters the species.

Ought this Sacrament to be made from Unleavened Bread?
(Q. 74, 4)

Two things are to be considered: (1) What is necessary? (2) What is becoming? It is necessary for bread to be wheaten; but not necessary to be leavened *only*, or unleavened; since it can be celebrated in either.

It is becoming however that every priest observe the rite of his Church. 'The Roman Church', says St Gregory, 'offered unleavened bread because our Lord took flesh without the union of the sexes.'

The Greek Church offered leavened bread, because the Word of the Father was clothed with flesh, as leaven is mixed with flour. Hence as a Latin priest sins by celebrating with fermented bread (as not pertaining to his rite), so a Greek priest sins by using unfermented bread as perverting the custom of his Church.

Obj. Leavened or unleavened are mere accidents of bread which do not change the species. But it makes no difference in Baptism whether the water used is salt or fresh, warm or cold; neither then should there be any distinction between unleavened and leavened bread, in the Eucharist.

Reply. The difference is greater between leavened and unleavened bread than that between hot and cold water; for what is fermented, retains an element of corruption; so there is the danger that the corruption of fermented bread may be such that it would not be valid matter.

Is the Wine of the Grape the proper matter of this Sacrament?
(Q. 74, 5)

Yes. Just as our Lord compared himself to the grain of wheat, so also did he compare himself to the vine, saying, '*I am the true vine*' (John 15, 1). But only bread from wheat is the matter of this sacrament (Art. 3). Therefore only wine from the grape is also the proper matter of the Eucharist, for three reasons:

First. Christ instituted it in wine from the grape (Matt. 26, 29).

Second. As said above (A3), the matter chosen in the sacraments is that which is in general use and regarded by all as belonging to a certain defined species. What comes from the grape is really wine: other liquors are simply called wine from their resemblance to the wine of the grape.

Third. Wine from the grape is more suited to the effect of this sacrament which is spiritual joy; because it is written: '*that wine may cheer the heart of man*' (Ps. 103, 15).

Obj. Pope Julius I rebukes priests for offering wine pressed from the grape:[1] therefore it seems that wine from the grape is not the proper matter.

Reply. In case of necessity it may be done, as Julius I

---

1 Decret. VII. This decree may refer to those tinged with montanist heresy, objecting to use of fermented wine. The Montanists were the Jansenists (or Puritans) of the early Church.

adds: 'If necessary let the grape be pressed into the chalice'; but the juice of unripe grapes has not the species of wine, and may not be used.

Should Water be mixed with the Wine? (Q. 74, 6)

It should: First, because it is believed that our Lord probably instituted this sacrament in wine mixed with water according to the custom of the country.

Secondly, it is in keeping with the representation of our Lord's Passion; for both blood and water flowed from his side.

Thirdly, it signifies the effect of the sacrament: 'When water is mixed with wine in the chalice', writes Pope Julius, 'the people are made one with Christ.'

Fourthly, St Ambrose says: 'The water flows into the chalice and springs into everlasting life.'

Obj. I. Bread and wine are the matter of this sacrament; nothing is added to the bread; neither should anything be added to the wine.

Reply. Bread is made of flour and water; therefore water is mixed with both bread and wine.

Is the mixing with Water essential? (Q. 74, 7)

No. We judge the sign by the thing signified: water is added to the wine to signify that the faithful share in this sacrament.

But this sacrament is completed by the consecration of the matter, whilst its use by the faithful is not an essential but only a consequence. Therefore adding the water is not essential.

Obj. Water flowed from our Lord's side as well as blood during the Passion of which this sacrament is a memorial: therefore water should be necessary as well as wine for this Sacrament.

Reply. The shedding of blood pertained directly to the Passion; for blood naturally flows from wounds. The flowing of water was not necessary for the Passion, but merely to show its effects, which are to wash away sins and protect us from the heat of concupiscence.

Should Water be added in great quantity? (Q. 74, 8)

It is always safer to add little water especially if the wine is weak; for the sacrament could not be celebrated if so much water was added as to destroy the species of the wine.

But what happens to the water that is added?

Some say the water remains by itself when the wine is changed into blood. Others say that as the wine is changed into blood, so the water is changed into the water that flowed from Christ's side.

Neither of these opinions can be held; because after the consecration there is nothing but the body of Christ; and if the water was changed into that which flowed from Christ, there would be a consecration of the wine, of the water, and of the bread; therefore, as Innocent III says: 'the more probable opinion is that the water is converted into wine and the wine into blood'.

Chapter III

THE CHANGE OF THE BREAD
AND WINE

*Is Christ's Body in this Sacrament in very truth or merely in
Figure or Sign?* (Q. 75, 1)

St Hilary says: 'There is no room for doubt according
to our Lord's own declaration and according to our
Faith, his flesh is truly meat and his blood is truly drink.'
(De Trin. VIII). And St Ambrose says: 'As the Lord
Jesus Christ is God's true Son so is it Christ's true flesh
which we receive.'

Christ's real presence cannot be detected by the sense,
or intellect but by faith alone resting on divine authority. Hence, commenting on the words *'This is my body'*
(Luke 22, 19), St Cyril says: *'Doubt not. Take the
Saviour's words with faith; since he is the Truth he lieth not.'*

These words: *'This is my body:'*—*'This is my blood:'*
prove first, the perfection of the New Law, secondly, his
love for us, and thirdly, the perfection of our faith.

First. They prove the perfection of the New Law, for
the sacrifices of the Old Law were only figures of the
true sacrifice of Christ's Passion. The sacrifice of the New
Law should have something more: it should contain
Christ, Christ himself, crucified, not merely in figure but
in very truth. It is therefore perfective of all the other
sacraments.

Second. They prove his love for us; for it is a special
mark of friendship to live together in closest intimacy:
'He that eateth my flesh and drinketh my blood abideth in

me and I in him'. Hence this sacrament is a sign of supreme charity, and the exaltation of our hope owing to such familiar union of Christ with us.

Third. They prove the perfection of our faith: For perfect faith has for its object the humanity of Christ as well as his divinity—according to St John (19, 12): '*You believe in God, believe also in me.*'

Now since faith is of things we do not see, and as Christ shows us his Godhead invisibly, so also in this sacrament does he show his flesh invisibly.

But shallow minds not looking closely into the truth of this mystery imagined that Christ's body and blood are not in this sacrament except in a sign; this is heretical and opposed to Christ's words—hence Berengarius, the first to confess the truth of what faith teaches.

St Thomas's four objections and replies are briefly as follows:

(1) When Augustine says :'You are not to eat this body which you see' he meant it was not to be eaten in the condition in which it was seen by the Jews: hence explaining the words '*The flesh profiteth nothing*' (John 5, 64) he says: 'They understood that the flesh was to be eaten as if it were a carcase that was cut up, or as it was sold in the market, not as it is quickened by the spirit.'

(2) When again Augustine says: 'The body in which he rose again must be in one place, his truth everywhere', he meant Christ's body as it is seen in its proper species,[1] just as our Lord says himself, 'But me thou hast not always' (Matt. 27, 11).

(3) 'No one can be in several places at the same time.' Christ's body is not in this sacrament as a body in a place with which it is commensurate, but in a special way proper to this sacrament. Hence we say that Christ's body

---

[1] As he is now in heaven or as he was visibly on earth.

is present on many altars, not as in different places but *sacramentally*.

(4) But the ruler was rebuked for demanding Christ's bodily presence; and the apostles were told they could not receive the Holy Ghost because they were so attached to our Lord's bodily presence. '*Except I go*', he says, '*the Paraclete will not come to you*' (John 16, 7).

Reply. All this refers to Christ's visible presence, but not as it is spiritually, that is invisibly in the manner and power of a spirit.

Does the substance of the Bread and Wine remain after Consecration? (Q. 75, 2)

No. 'Although the figures of the bread and wine be seen', says St Ambrose, 'still after consecration they are to be believed to be nothing else but the body and blood of Christ.'

Nothing can be where it was not previously, unless by change of place, or by conversion: For instance, a fire begins anew in a house either because it was carried there, or generated. Now Christ's body is in this sacrament *after* consecration but not before it. His body is not there by local motion. If it were, it would cease to be in heaven; for what moves from place to place must leave the one before it comes to the other; and it must move through all the intervening space: Now one and the same body cannot move and come to rest in different places at the one and the same time; whereas Christ's body under this sacrament begins to be in several places at the one and the same time. It follows then that the body of Christ cannot begin to exist in this sacrament unless by a change of the substance of bread into itself.

For, in the first place, what is changed into something else no longer remains; the substance of the bread therefore cannot remain after consecration.

Secondly. If the substance of the bread remained, it would not be true to say 'This is my body'; for the substance of the bread is never the body of Christ. One should say rather: 'Here is my body'.

Thirdly. If the substance of the bread remained, it would be adored as God alone is adored; and this would be opposed to the veneration of the sacrament, and also to the law of the Church which prohibits anyone from receiving the body of Christ after taking corporal nourishment, whilst it is lawful to take one consecrated host after another.

Is the substance of the Bread and Wine annihilated after consecration? (Q. 75, 3)

St Augustine says: 'God is not the cause of tending to nothingness.' Now this sacrament is due to divine power: therefore the substance of the bread or wine is not reduced to primary matter[1] or annihilated.

For, supposing the substance of the bread and wine were dissolved instead of being changed into the body and blood of Christ, such a dissolution would be perceived by the senses. Again, when could this dissolution take place? If you say at the last instant of consecration, then the substance of the body and blood of Christ is there together with the substance of the bread which is contrary to what is said above (Art. 2).

In the third place, supposing the substance of the bread and wine were annihilated, how did Christ's true body begin to be in this sacrament except by the change of the substance of bread into it? But this change is excluded the moment we admit either annihilation of the substance of

1 The primary matter in question is the simple elements which by their union (or composition) make, composed or mixed (non-simple) bodies. These elements were considered as themselves the primary matter. There is reference here to the physical (or chemical) science of St Thomas' day, when fire, air, earth and water were considered simple substances.

the bread or dissolution into its original matter. (For if no conversion there is no transubstantiation.)

Fourthly, no cause can be given for such dissolution or annihilation; for the *effect* of the sacrament is signified by these words of the form: '*This is my body.*'

Obj. I. Nothing is lost in nature. Whatever is corporeal must be somewhere; but this substance of the bread is corporeal and does not remain after consecration; and no one can say where it may be; therefore it is either annihilated, or dissolved.

Reply. It does not follow that it is dissolved, since it is changed into the body of Christ; just as it does not follow, if air be used to fan a fire and is not there or elsewhere, that it is therefore annihilated.

Obj. II. One of two contradictories must be true; but this proposition is false: 'After the consecration the substance of the bread and wine is something.' Therefore, this is true: 'The substance of the bread and wine is nothing.'

Reply. Although *after consecration*, the proposition 'The substance of the bread is something' is false: still, that into which the substance of the bread is changed is *something*; therefore the substance of the bread is not annihilated (but converted into the body of Christ).

Can Bread be converted into the Body of Christ? (Q. 75, 4)

Yes. 'To thee', says Eusebius of Emesa, 'it ought neither to be a novelty nor an impossibility that earthly things be changed into the substance of Christ.'

As Christ's body does not begin to be again in this sacrament by local motion or as in a place (as we have seen in the first and second article of this question) it must be said to begin there by conversion of the substance of bread into itself.

But this change is supernatural and due to God's power

alone. Hence St Ambrose says: 'It is clear that the Virgin conceived beyond the order of nature and *what we make is from the Virgin.*'

Every change made according to the laws of nature is a formal change (or a change of form), but God is an infinite Act (cf. P. 1, Q. VII, A. 1). Hence his actions embrace the whole order of being.

Therefore he can not only work *formal* conversions so that diverse forms succeed each other (as for instance water which exists in liquid, solid and gaseous forms), but he can also change all being so that the whole substance of one thing is changed into another.

This is done by divine power in this sacrament; for the whole substance of the bread and wine is changed[1] into the whole substance of the body and blood of Christ.

Hence this is not a formal but a substantial conversion which is not due to any natural movement; it therefore merits a name of its own, and may be called *transubstantiation.*

Obj. White never becomes black. As two contrary forms are of themselves diverse and are the principles of formal difference; so two signate matters [i.e., those expressed by a specific name—as, gold and silver] are of themselves diverse and are the principles of *material* distinction—therefore it is not possible for this matter of bread to become the matter whereby Christ's body is *individuated.*[2] So it is not possible for this substance

1 This is the word used in the Catechism. Strictly speaking it should be '*converted*'.
2 To individuate is to make individual, or numerically distinct, things within the same species.
   The principle of individuation is that which makes anything what it is and not some other thing of the same species. Hence an individual is one whose properties or peculiarities taken together cannot suit another—St Peter and St Andrew, although two brothers, are individually different. What individuates one man from another has been an age-long discussion. St Thomas says the principles of individuation are found in the material

of bread to be changed into the substance of Christ's body.

Reply. Matter cannot be changed into matter by the power of any finite agent or form into form. Such a change can only be accomplished by an infinite agent which controls all being. [For instance God alone can change silver into gold. Each metal consists of matter and form. Matter is that which is indifferent to constitute this thing or that thing. But what determines and perfects matter is called form; and it is because of *this* form that *this* thing is called gold or *that* thing is called silver.[1]]

Do the accidents of the Bread and Wine remain in this Sacrament after the change? (Q. 75, 5)

Yes. St Augustine says, 'Under the species (or appearances) which we see of bread and wine we honour invisible things, namely, flesh and blood.'

It is evident to the senses that all the accidents of bread and wine remain after consecration. Divine providence arranged this and reasonably:

First, because it would be horrible to eat human flesh, and drink visible human blood. Therefore Christ's flesh and blood are set before us under the species of things commonly used by men. Secondly, that while we receive our Lord's body and blood invisibly, it may increase the merit of our faith.[2]

part of our nature. It is the foundation but not the whole principle. The form (as for instance the human soul) is also a co-principle, but it is such by reason of the matter with which it is united. As the angels are pure forms and absolutely devoid of matter. St Thomas holds that each must be a distinct species, otherwise there would be nothing to distinguish one from the other (cf. 1, 76, 2 ad 2 and 1, 50, 4). (See Appendix IV.)

1 This is the answer to the third objection. The first two (omitted) refer to formal changes such as food changed into flesh or air into fire—not to changes of the entire substance which St Thomas calls Conversion.

2 Another reason given is that if our Lord were eaten as he is now in heaven (*sub propria specie*) infidels would only mock this sacrament. It could happen that non-believers would sometimes be struck with terror if our Lord appeared in his own proper species.

C

Obj. I. Substance is naturally before accidents: when that which comes first is removed, what follows is taken away; therefore accidents should not remain.

Reply. An effect depends more upon the first cause than upon the second. God is the first cause of all things. By his power it is possible for that which follows to remain, whilst that which comes first is taken away.

Obj. II. There ought to be no deception in the sacrament of truth. But we judge substances by accidents. Here human judgment seems to be deceived if, while the accidents remain, the substance does not remain.

Reply. There is no deception; for the accidents we see are truly present; but the intellect whose proper object is substance, is preserved from deception by faith, and by the clear and unmistakable words of our Lord himself when he instituted this sacrament. Hence St Thomas's own words:

'Visus, tactus, gustus in Te fallitur
Sed auditu solo tuto creditur.'
'The sight, the touch, the taste, these all deceive,
The ear alone securely I believe.'

Does the substantial form[1] of the bread remain after the Consecration? (Q. 75, 6)

No. If it did, the matter of the bread would be changed, not into the whole body of Christ, but only into its matter and this would be opposed to the words of the form: '*This is my body.*'

Secondly. If the substantial form remained, it would be either in matter or apart from matter: If in matter, the whole substance of the bread would remain; for it cannot

[1] Substantial form is that principle which determines and perfects matter and makes it a complete substance of a particular species; as for instance, the substantial form of bread is that which makes this thing called bread and not something else. See reply to objection on page 22.

be in any other matter, since a proper form is only in its proper matter.

If apart from matter, that is, suppose the substantial form of the bread was separated from the pure material of the bread, with which it should be naturally united: this form would be an actual intelligence;[1] because if a form could exist apart from matter it would be such.

Thirdly, it would not be becoming to this sacrament. For all the accidents remain, that the body of Christ may be seen under them (by the eyes of faith) and not under its *proper* species.

Obj. I. Bread is an artificial thing; therefore its form is an accident and remains after consecration.

Reply. Art can produce substantial forms that are not accidents (for instance a brass frog or serpent) not by the power of art itself, but by the power of natural energies— as for example the substantial form of bread is due to the action of fire, and the matter to the mixing of the flour and water.

Obj. II. The form of Christ's body is his soul. But the substantial form of bread is not changed into his soul. Therefore it remains after consecration.

Reply. But the soul is the form of the body since it gives perfect being, namely corporeal being and animated being. But the form of bread is changed into Christ's body according to as it gives corporeal but not animated being.

1 St Thomas means that only a form which is an intellect is such that it can exist apart from matter. This is because only such forms are separable from matter: hence they alone can exist apart. Forms which are less perfect are more dependent on matter. They have not that degree of immateriality which permits separate existence. None lower than the intellect has this. The form, say, of gold or silver cannot even by a miracle exist apart from matter. Were it such that it could, it would be an intellect.

Immateriality and intelligence go together and are shared in different degrees, e.g. men and angels. And immateriality which is such that it can exist apart from matter is called spirit. The purely material is *prima materia*— it cannot exist as such.

Obj. III. The peculiar operations of anything follows its substantial form. But what remains in this sacrament nourishes and performs every operation as bread would, if present. Therefore the substantial form of bread remains after consecration.

Reply. Some of the operations of the bread follow it by reason of the accidents and some operations are bestowed miraculously as will be seen later.[1] (cf. 77, Art. 3.)

Is this change instantaneous? (Q. 75, 7)

Yes. The power that effects it is infinite and it belongs to that power to work in an instant.

A change may be instantaneous on the part of the form, on the part of the subject, and on the part of the agent.

First. If it be a form that receives more or less, the change is successive, such as health. But a substantial form does not receive more or less; therefore its introduction into matter is instantaneous.

Secondly, if it is on the part of the subject: sometimes it is prepared gradually to receive the form just as water is heated. But when the subject is in its final disposition to receive the form, then it acquires it suddenly, such as glass when illumined.

Thirdly, on the part of the agent whose power is infinite: St Mark writes when Christ said *ephpheta* which is '*be thou opened*' *immediately his ears were opened and the string of his tongue loosed.* [7. 34.]

For three reasons therefore, this conversion is instantaneous: First, because Christ's body is the term of conversion and does not receive more or less. Secondly, the subject is not disposed successively; and thirdly it is effected by infinite power.

Obj. I. This change must occur according to the suc-

---

1 The same holds for the accidents of the wine, such as power of intoxicating, of heating, etc.

cession of time which is between the last instant[1] in which the bread was there and the first instant in which the Body is present.

Reply. Time is not made up of successive instants;[2] therefore a *first instant* can be assigned in which Christ's body is present but only a *last time* can be assigned when the bread was there. The same holds in natural changes.

Obj. II. St Ambrose says that *this sacrament is made by the words of Christ.* But Christ's words are pronounced successively.

Reply. The change comes to pass in the last instant of the pronouncing of the words. Their meaning is then finished and its efficaciousness in the forms of the sacraments; therefore it does not follow that this is successive.

Is this proposition false: The Body of Christ is made of Bread? (Q. 75, 8)

No. For St Ambrose says: '*When consecration takes place, the body of Christ is made out of bread.*'

That is provided the preposition used to express 'out of' is *ex* and not *de* which St Ambrose uses here, but really means *ex* which denotes order.

St Thomas's explanation is lengthy and technical. Briefly it is this:

Bread and the body of Christ are two extremes in the supernatural order, just as black and white are in the natural order; and when one extreme is changed into the other, conversion is common to both orders. But although one extreme follows the other, they cannot exist together. So we may not say white is black.

---

1 An 'instant' is the indivisible point of duration.

2 Time is the particular instant between the one that is just past and the one that is yet to come. Hence it is not made up of successive instants. Its totality, past, present, and future, only exist in the mind; for the past is gone and the future yet to come. Therefore, Aristotle says: 'If there was no mind there would be no time.'

In creation there are extremes but no conversion, because nothingness cannot be a subject of conversion [and by subject here is meant something in which a change takes place].

But as we can say 'The world is made of nothing', meaning that material existence follows non-existence yet is not due to it: so also we may say, 'The body of Christ is made from bread', yet with this difference; that in the latter case there is a conversion of one substance into another; and the change is called *transubstantiation*. In this sense only, is the body of Christ said to be *made out of bread*.

But we cannot say the body of Christ is made from bread if we use the Latin preposition *de* (from) because *de*[1] denotes a consubstantial cause. Still, as the accidents of bread remain the same in this sacrament after the change, some of these expressions may be admitted by way of similitude, as for instance 'Bread is the body of Christ' or 'The Body of Christ is made of bread' provided that by the word *bread* is *not* meant the substance of bread, but that under these species there is first contained the substance of bread and afterwards the body of Christ.

Obj. I. This proposition is false. 'Bread can be the body of Christ.' Therefore it is also false to say 'The body of Christ is made out of bread.'

Reply. Potentiality belongs to the subject. But there is no subject in this conversion; for it is not effected by the *passive potentiality*[2] of the creature, but solely by the *active* power of the Creator.

---

1 For instance, in the words 'Qui conceptus est de Spiritu Sancto' (who was conceived by the Holy Ghost), *de* denotes the consubstantial cause: The three persons of the Blessed Trinity co-operated in the virginal conception, but it is attributed to the Holy Ghost, because he is the Love of the Father and the Son and the Incarnation is due to the supreme Love of God (*Summa* III, Q. 33, Art. I).

2 Passive potentiality of the creature may be illustrated by water when affected by heat or cold, turning into vapour or ice.

Obj. II. This proposition seems to be false: 'The bread is converted into the body of Christ'—because such a conversion, in which it is not said that non-being is converted into being, appears to be more miraculous than the creation of the world. Therefore the proposition: 'The body of Christ is made out of bread' seems also to be false.

Reply. In this change there are many more difficulties than in creation. In creation there was but one difficulty— how something is made out of nothing. But in this conversion one whole is changed into another whole, so that nothing remains of the first; and a further difficulty is that the accidents remain while the substance ceases to be,[1] and yet the word *conversion* is admitted in this sacrament but not in creation.

1 St Thomas's words are *corruptâ substantiâ.*

INTRODUCTORY NOTE TO
CHAPTER IV

IN the following articles St Thomas refers to extension and quantity.

The very idea of a material body implies parts beyond parts or extension. It must be a certain length, breadth, depth or height. That is dimensive quantity or something which can be measured and applies only to corporeal things (1, 42, 1 ad 1).

Quantity can be increased or decreased and in this way is opposed to substance which of itself cannot be increased or decreased (1a, 2a, 52, 1).

For we know for instance that the substance of bread is just as *completely* in a crumb as in a loaf—since substance of itself is not subject to degrees.

In the Blessed Sacrament the quantity of our Lord's body is there, but not in a way quantity is usually present. That is, it is not there after the manner of dimensions but it is inseparable from its substance and exists without extension of parts. So that the visible dimensive quantity we see is that of the bread and wine; and it is the primary accident in which all other accidents inhere such as taste, colour, shape, etc., or in other words it is the subject of all other accidents.

By a subject is meant that in which something else exists. Accidents (apart from the miracle of the Blessed Eucharist) always inhere in *a substance ultimately*. Quantity is not only the *immediate subject*, but it is a subject *which itself inheres in substance:* all accidents inhere in substance but through the *medium of quantity*.

CHAPTER IV

HOW CHRIST IS IN THIS SACRAMENT

Is the whole Christ contained under this Sacrament? (Q. 76, 1)
[By the whole Christ is meant his integral body, blood,
soul and divinity, viz. the Person of the Word.[1]]

The entire Christ is in this sacrament, first, by power of
the sacrament, secondly by concomitance.[2]

By power of the sacrament there is under the species
(or appearances) that which is expressed by the words of
the form: '*This is my body*'—'*This is my blood.*'

From natural concomitance there is also that which is
really united to the body and blood. (Namely, the soul
of Christ and his divinity.)

In a real union of two things, where one is, the other
must be; and they are only distinguished by an operation
of the mind.

Obj. I. The bread and wine cannot be changed into
either the divinity or soul of Christ; therefore it seems
that the entire Christ is not under this sacrament.

Reply. Where the body of Christ is, there the Godhead
must be; for once the body was assumed by the divinity,
it is never set aside. But his soul was truly separated from
his body; so if this sacrament had been effected during
those three days, the soul of Christ would not have been

---

1 Ubiquitarians such as Apollinarists and Eutychians confused the two natures
of Christ and taught that Christ as man was everywhere (*ubique*).

2 By concomitance here is meant what must be present by nature or by
virtue of the grace of union. In the Host the blood is present by concomitance
and in the chalice, the body, as one cannot be without the other after the
Resurrection; and by concomitance the divinity must be united to both.

there either by power of the sacrament or from real concomitance. Now since 'Christ rising from the dead dieth
now no more' (Rom. 6, 9), his soul is always really
united with his body and is present in this sacrament by
real concomitance.

Obj. II. This sacrament consists of food and drink
(cf. 74, 1), but our Lord said: 'My flesh is meat indeed,
and my blood is drink indeed.' Therefore only the
flesh and blood of Christ are present. But there are other
parts of Christ's body such as nerves, bones, sinews;
therefore the entire body of Christ is not contained under
this sacrament.

Reply. The form of this sacrament is not: 'This is my
flesh' but '*This is my body.*' Therefore not only the flesh
but the whole body of Christ is present; that is, every
bone, nerve, sinew, etc. So when our Lord said '*My flesh
is meat indeed*', the word *flesh* is put for the entire body.

Obj. III. A body of greater quantity cannot be contained under the measure of a lesser. But the measure of
bread and wine is much smaller than the measure of
Christ's body; therefore it is impossible for the entire
Christ to be contained under this sacrament.

Reply. The body of Christ is in this sacrament by *way
of substance* and not by way of quantity. But the proper
Totality[1] of substance is contained in a small equally as
well as in a large quantity, just as the whole nature of air
is contained in a large or small amount of air, and the
whole nature in every man whether he be big or small.
Therefore the whole substance of Christ's body and blood
is contained in this sacrament after consecration just as
the whole substance of the bread and wine was there
before consecration.

1 The whole substance of bread is contained as much in a crumb as in a whole
loaf. Simply the loaf has greater quantity.

Is the whole Christ contained under each species of this Sacrament? (Q. 76, 2)

Yes. The gloss[1] on the word 'chalice' (1 Cor. 11, 2) says 'The same is received under each species.' The whole Christ is certainly under the one and the other sacramental species or appearances: His body is under the appearance of bread by power of the sacrament, his blood from real concomitance, and so also his soul and divinity.

But *vice versa*, his blood is under the appearance of wine by power of the sacrament, and his body and soul and divinity by real concomitance: for his body and blood are not separated now as they were at his death on the cross. But if this sacrament had been consecrated then, the body would have been without the blood under the appearance of bread, and the blood without the body under the appearance of wine.

Obj. I. Nothing is contained under one species that is not contained under the other; one of them therefore seems superfluous.

Reply. Although the whole Christ is under each species, it is not without good reasons that he is whole and entire in both: first, to represent his Passion in which the body and blood were separated: hence in the form for consecration of the wine the shedding of blood is mentioned. Secondly, it suits the *use* of this sacrament that Christ's body and blood should be shown apart, as food and drink. Thirdly, it suits its *effect*; for, as said above (74, 1) the body is offered for the salvation of the body, and the blood for the salvation of the soul.

---

1 The 'gloss' here referred to was a favourite commentary on the Scriptures from the ninth to the seventeenth century, compiled by Strabo, a German, born 807 and regarded by St Thomas as a high authority.

Is Christ under every part of the species of the Bread and Wine?
(Q. 76, 3)

St Augustine says: 'Each receives Christ, the Lord, who is entire under every portion. Nor is he any less in each but gives himself entire in every morsel.' (Gregorian Sacramentary.)

Christ's body is in the sacrament *substantively*, namely, in the way in which substance is *under* dimension, but not *after* the manner of dimension.

That is to say, Christ's body is not present in the way in which the dimensive quantity of a body is under the dimensive quantity of place.

The whole nature of substance is under every part of the dimensions under which it is contained. Just as the whole nature of air is under every part of the atmosphere, and the entire nature of bread under every particle of bread whether divided or undivided, so Christ is under every part of the species of the bread even while the Host remains entire and not merely when broken.

Some explain this by the single image that appears in an unbroken mirror. The comparison is not perfect; for the multiplied images result from the various reflections in the various parts of the broken mirror. But here there is only one[1] consecration whereby Christ's body is in this sacrament.

Obj. I. If Christ be entirely under every part of the species, he would be an infinite number of times in this sacrament, which is unreasonable; because the infinite is repugnant to grace[2] as well as to nature.

---

1 See Q. 73, Art. 2, P. 8, where St Thomas says '*Materially* consecration is two-fold, but in all other respects, *formally* and *perfectively* one.' Hence the words of the Catechism: 'The bread and wine are changed into the body and blood of our Lord at *the* consecration.'

2 By grace here is meant *created* grace. *Increated* grace is God himself—the merits of Christ are said to be infinite, because the person who merited was

Reply. Number follows division. As long as quantity remains actually undivided, the entire substance of anything is not several times under its dimensions; therefore, neither is Christ's body several times under the dimensions of the species of the bread, nor present an infinite number of times, but just as many as it is divided into parts.

Obj. II. Christ's body is organic. There must be determinate distance between various parts, eye and eye, eye and ear. But if he is entire under every part of the species —where one part of the body is, another would be there also.

Reply. The determinate distance of parts in an organic body rests on dimensive quantity. But the nature of substance precedes even dimensive quantity and since Christ is properly and directly in this sacrament according to the manner of substance—such distance of parts which are in Christ's body (in its proper species) is not computed in this sacrament, according to that distance but after the manner of its substance.

Is the whole dimensive quantity of Christ's Body in this Sacrament? (Q. 76, 4)

Yes. According to its being, the dimensive quantity of any body is not separated from its substance.[1] But the entire substance of Christ's body is present in this sacrament (cf. 76, 1), so also its entire dimensive quantity.

As said above, any part of Christ's body is in this sacrament in two ways: (*a*) by the power of the sacrament; (*b*) by real concomitance.

God—but the plenitude of *created* grace which Christ has as man is not infinite (cf. Suarez De Myst. Vit. Christi D. 18, Sec. IV).

[1] This is according to Marietti's edition, viz., Quantitas dimensiva corporis alicujus non separatur secundum esse a substantia ejus. The Dominican translation of the Leonine edition reads: The existence of the dimensive quantity of any body *cannot* be separated from the existence of its substance.

The conversion which occurs in this sacrament is terminated directly at the substance of Christ's body, and not at its dimensions. So they are present only from real concomitance, as is evident from the fact that the dimensive quantity of the bread remains: whilst only the substance of the bread passes away.

Obj. I. Two dimensive quantities cannot be present together in the same subject.

Reply. Two dimensive quantities cannot naturally be in the same subject at the same time. But in this sacrament the dimensive quantity is there after its proper manner, that is, according to commensuration (or to the self-same extent or capacity the bread and wine had before consecration): not so the dimensive quantity of Christ's body; it is only there after the manner of substance.

Obj. II. The whole body of Christ is under each particle of the consecrated Host. But no dimensive quantity is entirely in any whole, and in its every part; therefore it is impossible for the whole dimensive quantity of Christ's body to be contained in this sacrament.

Reply. We determine how a thing exists by what belongs to it, of itself, not by what is accidentally united to it. An object, for instance, exists in the retina of the eye according as it is white—not according as it is sweet; though it may be both white and sweet. Hence sweetness is in the sight after the manner of whiteness. In the same way, the substance of the body of Christ is present on the altar by virtue of the sacrament, whilst its dimensive quantity is there by concomitance, or as it were accidentally. Therefore it is present not in its proper way, namely, whole in whole, part in part, but after the manner of substance whose nature is to be whole in the whole, and whole in every part.

Obj. III. As the dimensive quantity of Christ's body is

much larger than that of the Host, then even the substance of Christ's body will be outside the species of the bread.

Reply. The dimensive quantity of our Lord's body is not in this sacrament in the way peculiar to quantity, by which the greater is beyond the lesser; but is there in the way mentioned above.

Introduction to Q. 76, 5

St Thomas teaches in this article that Christ is not in the Eucharist as in a place.

If by place is meant to be really somewhere, then the body of Christ is present in the Blessed Eucharist wherever the species are, as the Council of Trent teaches. (Sess. XIII, C. X.)

But if we mean by a place some definite part of space, then Christ is not present in the sacred species so that one portion of his body is at one point and another at another, as for instance he is in Heaven.

For Christ's body is in the Eucharist without any extension of parts: or in other words it is there by way of substance: no substance, not even a corporeal substance, fills any definite part of space or place, if the action of quantity, which cannot exist without extension of parts, be suspended. This action is suspended by miracle in the Blessed Sacrament where the quantity of Christ's body exists without any extension whatsoever; and hence is said to be intrinsic (Q. 76, 5 ad. 3).

Is Christ's Body in this Sacrament as in a place? (Q. 76, 5)

No. First, because place and object must be equal. But the place where this sacrament is, is much smaller than the body of Christ, therefore Christ's body is not in this sacrament as in a place. If Christ's body were present according to its proper dimensions, it must be commensurate with the place according to its dimensive quantity.

(That is, according to its own length, breadth, etc.) But it is not present in this way, but rather after the manner of substance, whose nature is for the whole to be in the whole and whole in every part: hence the body of Christ is not in this sacrament as in a place.

Secondly. Because the substance of Christ's body succeeds the substance of the bread. But the substance of the bread was not locally under its dimensions, but after the manner of substances; so neither is the substance of Christ's body.

Again by reason of its own dimensions, the substance of the bread was there locally, because it was related to that place through the medium of its own dimensions: but the substance of Christ's body is computed through the medium of dimensions that are not its own.

Hence, the proper dimensions of Christ's body are compared with that place through the medium of substance which is contrary to the notion of a located body: therefore in no way is Christ's body locally in this sacrament.

Obj. I. It belongs to being in a place to be there *definitely* (as the soul is in the body) or circumscriptively (i.e., where parts of the body correspond to parts of space). But Christ is so present where the species of bread and wine are, that he is nowhere else on the altar. Therefore his body seems to be *definitely* in this sacrament. Again, it seems to be circumscriptively present since it is so contained under the species of the consecrated Host, that it neither exceeds it nor is exceeded by it.

Reply. If Christ's body was *definitely* on the altar it would only be on one particular altar where this sacrament is consecrated; but it is in Heaven under its own species, and on many altars under the sacramental species. Again, it is not under this sacrament circumscriptively, for it is not there according to the commensuration of its quantity. (In other words its proper parts do not correspond with the parts of the Host, or with those of the precious blood. But Christ's body is in both *indivisibly*, that is, whole and entire in the whole Host and in the chalice. Necessarily the dimensive quantity of Christ's body exists in the same way.)

Obj. II. Whatever fills a place is there locally. The substance of bread is not there, but the body of Christ is; therefore it is locally present; if not, the place would be empty: and nature abhors a vacuum.

Reply. The place is filled with the sacramental species, either because of the nature of dimensions, or at least miraculously, since they subsist miraculously.

Obj. III. 'There' and 'thence' are numbered among the nine kinds of accidents: But Christ's body is in this sacrament with all its accidents; therefore Christ's body is locally present in it.

Reply. The accidents of Christ's body are present by real concomitance, not by power of the Sacrament. Therefore they are *intrinsic*[1] to it. To be in a place is an accident compared with its extrinsic container. Therefore Christ need not be in this sacrament as in a place.

Introduction to Q. 76, 6

It may be asked why did St Thomas hold that our Lord is not movable in the Blessed Sacrament because

---

[1] St Thomas here distinguishes internal (intrinsic) and external (extrinsic) place. He says the former (intrinsic) is present but not the latter.

Internal Place: The internal accident which situates a substance.

External Place: The surface of the containing body (cf. Phys. Lib. 4, C. 4; Quodlib. 6, Q. 2, Art. 3).

An example of an *internal* place would be the stone of the sepulchre, or wall of the cenacle, or the womb of the Virgin at the moment our Lord passed through them. (Cf. Supplement, Q. 83, 2.)

'That body of our Lord', says St Gregory, 'entered into the company of disciples through closed doors, which to human eyes by his nativity went forth from the Virgin's womb.'

D

he is there by way of substance and without extrinsic dimensive quantity, whilst the angels who are pure immaterial substances without any dimensive quantity whatsoever are said to be movable? [1, 53].

The fact that an angel can descend from Heaven to earth or go to the furthest star involves no contradiction as would happen in the case of our Lord. For if he came into the Blessed Sacrament in a movable way he would have one set of predicates attaching him as *here* in this Blessed Sacrament and another set *there* in another tabernacle and yet another in a third, fourth . . . twentieth tabernacle and still a further set as abiding all the time in Heaven.

Hence St Thomas holds our Lord is not movable in the Blessed Sacrament. But with the angels it is not really local motion which is properly only possible to beings that are circumscriptively in a place, that is, to those whose bodies correspond to parts in space. Again, Christ is subject to no change whatever, for example, to that of ceasing to be here present after a certain time. He remains as long as the species are incorrupt, which could be for months, even years, especially if the species are not exposed to the air.

Is Christ's Body movable in this Sacrament? (Q. 76, 6)

No. The same thing cannot be in motion and at rest at the same time; otherwise there is contradiction in the same subject.

As Christ is not present in this sacrament as in a place, he is not moved locally of himself but accidentally; that is, by the motion of what he is under, the appearances of bread or wine. They only can be actually moved.

The reason given by St Thomas may be illustrated by an object that is white and large: it can be made black and still remain the same size. The object then is immovable as to size, and movable as to colour; for the same reason Christ is the same in Heaven and in this sacrament as regards substance; but he does not exist in the same way for in Heaven his body is in a place where its parts correspond to their surrounding medium; but in this sacrament they do not; as they only exist in it after the manner of substance.

Again, whatever possesses unfailing existence of itself cannot be the principle of failing; existence when Christ ceases to be under this sacrament, it is not because he ceases to be, nor yet by a local motion of his own but only because the sacramental species cease to exist.[1]

Obj. I. Aristotle says: 'When we are moved the things within us are moved.' This is true even of the human soul although a spiritual substance.

But Christ is in this sacrament as shown above (76, 1) therefore when the Blessed Sacrament is moved Christ is moved.

Reply. Since Christ is not in this sacrament as in a place, he is only moved accidentally as said above.

Obj. II. Nothing was to remain of the paschal lamb until the morning (Exodus 12, 19). But the paschal lamb was a figure of this sacrament—therefore Christ will not be present if the sacrament is reserved until morning, and so is not immovably in this sacrament.

Reply. Some influenced by this argument imagined that Christ's body does not remain under this sacrament

1 CHRIST AS GOD: Always being born, never can cease to exist.

CHRIST AS MAN: Once born, once ceased to exist as man, when body and soul were separated on the cross—but never again when re-united in the Resurrection (III, 50, 4).

CHRIST AS VICTIM: Always being born as Victim, so to speak, at the consecration; always ceasing as such when the sacramental species are dissolved in one place, only to begin anew on another altar.

But when Christ ceased to be Man on the Cross, his divinity remained united to his soul and body, hence we say: 'Christ descended into hell', i.e., his soul: Christ was buried, i.e. his body.

if kept to the morning. St Cyril writes of these: 'Some are so bereft of reason as to say that the mystical blessing departs from the sanctification (i.e. the sacrament) if any of it remain to the next day. For Christ's consecrated body is not changed, but the power of the blessing and the life-giving grace is perpetually in it.' Although the Truth corresponds to the figure, the figure cannot equal it.

Obj. III. Christ does not remain in this sacrament for all time; therefore it seems that Christ is movably in the sacrament.

Reply. Christ remains so long as the sacramental species remain. When they cease Christ's body ceases to be under them, but not because it depends on them but because the relationship of Christ's body to these species is taken away. In this way God ceases to be the Lord of a creature when it ceases to exist.

Can the Body of Christ as it exists in this Sacrament be seen by any eye or at least by one that is glorified? (Q. 76, 7)

No. Anything remaining the same cannot be seen by the same eye in different appearances at the same time. But the glorified eye always sees Christ as he is in his own species according to Isaias: '*His eyes shall see the king in his beauty*' (33, 7). It seems then that the glorified eye does not see Christ as he is under the sacramental species.

The eye is of two kinds, the bodily eye and the intellectual eye, so called by similitude. The bodily eye cannot see Christ's body, first, because its accidents are not visible, and secondly because it is present by way of substance in this sacrament. But a substance as such is not visible to bodily eye nor does it come under the senses nor even under the imagination, but only under the intellect whose object is *What a thing is* (De Anima III) and therefore is called the *spiritual eye*.

Since Christ's presence is wholly supernatural in this sacrament, he can only be seen by a beatified intellect of man or angel through the participated glory of the divine intellect in the vision of the divine essence.

But here by wayfarers, he can only be seen by faith: not even the angelic intellect by its own power can behold him.

Therefore the demons cannot by their intellect perceive Christ in this sacrament except through faith, to which they do not willingly assent. Yet they are convinced of his presence from the evidence of signs, according to St James, '*The devils believe and tremble*' (1, 19).

Obj. I. The glorified body of the saints will be *made like to the glory of Christ's body*. But Christ's eye beholds himself as he is in this sacrament: Therefore for the same reason every other glorified eye can see him.

Reply. Christ's own bodily eye sees himself under the sacrament, yet not the way in which he exists there; because that belongs to the intellect. It is not so with another glorified eye, since Christ's eye is under this sacrament in a way in which no other glorified eye is conformed to it.

Is Christ's Body truly there when flesh or a child miraculously appears in this Sacrament? (Q. 76, 8)

Yes. For the same reverence is shown to what appears as was exhibited at first and no such reverence of *latria* would be paid if Christ were not really there.

Such an apparition may happen in two ways. First, to one person this sacrament is seen under the appearance of flesh or of a child, whilst to others it is seen under the appearance of bread.

There is no deception here as practised by magicians: because such a species is divinely formed in the eye to show that Christ's body is really under the sacrament—

just as Christ appeared without deception to the disciples going to Emmaus.

Since there was no change in the sacrament, it is plain that when such apparitions do occur, Christ does not cease to be under this sacrament.

Secondly, sometimes such an apparition remains not for an hour but for a considerable time and not merely by a change wrought in the beholders but by an appearance that exists outwardly. Some think that it is the proper species of Christ's body, or at least a part of his flesh; because it is in the power of a glorified body to be seen by a non-glorified eye either entirely or in part and under its own semblance or in a strange guise as will be seen later.

This seems unlikely: first, because Christ's body can be seen only in one place under its proper species, namely in Heaven. Secondly, because a glorified body appears and disappears at will: St Luke says: 'Our Lord vanished out of the sight of the disciples.' (24, 31.) But what appears in this sacrament under the likeness of flesh continues for a long time; and we read of its being enclosed in a pyx by the order of many bishops, which would be wicked to think of doing were Christ under his proper species.

Obj. Christ's body begins to be in this sacrament by consecration and conversion. But the flesh and blood which appear by miracle are not consecrated or changed into Christ's true body and blood, therefore the body or the blood of Christ is not under these species.

Reply. The dimensions of the consecrated bread and wine continue while a miraculous change is wrought in its other accidents (such as colour, shape, smoothness, etc., as said above in Q. 75, 5).

INTRODUCTION TO CHAPTER V

WE have seen in the introduction what is meant by an accident and subject. In this chapter reference is made to 'universal' accidents—to understand what these exactly mean a few words must be added on *Attention* and *Abstraction*.

Universal accidents are those which are not applied to any subject in particular as 'light', 'hard', 'heavy', 'soft', 'black', 'white', but when applied to certain substances, as for instance the word 'fresh' to water, 'incorruptible' to cedar, then they become individual and sensible.

But why call then 'universal'? In handbooks of philosophy *Attention* and *Abstraction* are discussed together and necessarily so. An example will best explain what they mean. I take, say, a feather and notice it is *light*, and I pass over its shape, size, colour. This *noticing* or aspect is ATTENTION.

From the feeling that the feather is light and from what I know about other substances, such as air, gossamer, cork, etc., I gather the general idea of lightness; and this is ABSTRACTION. That is: the intellect expresses in a universal form the individual 'accident light' which it seizes and knows. But to know is to free from matter, and therefore to universalize. Thus we have the (universal) abstract noun 'lightness' or a universal accident. See also p. 49, note on abstraction.

CHAPTER V

HOW THE ACCIDENTS REMAIN IN
THE EUCHARIST

Do the accidents remain without a subject in this Sacrament?
(Q. 77, 1)

YES. St Gregory says: 'The sacramental species are the
names of those things which were before (consecration)': namely, those accidents of bread and wine. The
species of the bread and wine that we perceive after consecration cannot have the substance of the bread and wine
of their substantial form for a subject, because neither the
substance nor the substantial form remains.

Again, these accidents or species do not abide in the
substance of Christ's body and blood because the substance of a human body can in no way be affected by
them. Nor can the glorious and impassible body of Christ
be so altered as to receive these qualities.

But some say that they are in the surrounding atmosphere as in a subject. This cannot be; first, because air is
not susceptive of such accidents, and secondly, because air
is displaced by them; thirdly, because accidents are
numerically one with the subject to which they are naturally united. Hence they cannot pass to another subject
and remain the same identical accidents. Finally, since air
is not deprived of its own accidents, it would have both
these and extraneous accidents at one and the same
time.

It cannot even be said that this is done miraculously by
virtue of the words of consecration; for they do not

signify this but only effect what they signify. It follows then that the accidents remain in this sacrament without a subject. This can be done by divine power, for God is the first cause of both substance and accident; and by his infinite power can preserve accidents in existence when the substance is withdrawn by virtue of which they naturally existed.

For just as he formed a human body in the Virgin's womb without the seed of man, so also he can produce any other effect he likes without any co-operation of their natural causes.

Obj. I. It is against the order established by God for accidents to be without a subject (as weight for instance to exists without matter) and it seems also like deceitfulness, since accidents naturally tell us what the subject is (as for instance cold discovers the iceberg which is the subject in which cold exists and from which it radiates).

Reply. On account of the reasons given in Question 75 (Article 5), the accidents of the bread and wine (colour, taste, form, etc.), exist without their subjects (bread and wine) after these substances are changed into the body and blood of Christ. For there is nothing to prevent the law of grace from ordaining a thing that is contrary to the law of nature as raising the dead or restoring sight to the blind.

Obj. II. Not even by a miracle can a definition be separated from the thing defined. For instance a man is defined as a rational animal and cannot be irrational and remain a man, otherwise contradictories would exist together in the same subject.

Now a definition of anything is what its name signifies. An accident from its very name 'falls on' or inheres in something else; whilst a substance subsists of itself and not in another substance. Therefore not even by a miracle can accidents exist in this sacrament without a subject.

Reply. Since being is not a genus, being or existence is therefore not the essence of either substance or accident (as something more defined is needed) therefore the definition of a substance is not 'a being of itself without a subject', nor the definition of an accident 'a being in a subject'. But it belongs to the essence of a substance *to have existence not in a subject*, while it belongs to the essence of an accident *to have existence in a subject*.

But in this sacrament it is not by virtue of their essence that accidents are not in a subject, but through divine power which sustains them. Therefore they do not cease to be accidents; for the definition of an accident is not withdrawn from them, which is an aptitude for a subject, nor does the definition of a substance apply to them.

Obj. III. Accidents are individuated[1] by their subject. If they remain accidents without a subject in this sacrament they will not be individual but universal, which would be evidently false because they would thus not be sensible but merely intelligible; therefore if they exist at all it must be in a subject.

Reply. When the substance of the bread and wine is changed into the body and blood of Christ these accidents remain in the individuated being they had previously possessed; hence they are singular and sensible, and continue to exist by divine power without a subject.

Obj. IV. But if the accidents remain without a subject after consecration they are simpler than angels which is unreasonable since these accidents are perceptible to the senses.

Reply. As long as the substance of the bread and wine remained, their accidents had no being of their own, but their subjects (that is, the substance of the bread and wine)

1 See note on page 22.

had being of this kind through them, just as snow is white through whiteness. But after consecration these accidents have being: hence they are composed of existence (*esse*) and essence (*quod est*) as was said of the angels; and along with that they have a further composition that belongs to parts that have quantity.

Is the dimensive quantity of the Bread or Wine the subject of the other accidents? (Q. 77, 2)

Yes. Qualities (being accidents) are only accidentally divisible by reason of the subject. Our senses tell us that they are divided in this sacrament only when the dimensive quantity is divided; therefore dimensive quantity is that in which inhere the other accidents that remain.

First, because something having quantity and colour and other accidents is perceived by the senses. Secondly, because the first disposition of matter is dimensive quantity. Hence Plato assigned *great and small* as the first difference of matter. Now since the first subject is matter, and dimensive quantity the first disposition of matter, then all these accidents are related to their subject through dimensive quantity, just as surface is the first subject of colour; and since, when the subject is withdrawn, the accidents remain as they were before, it follows that all the accidents remain founded on dimensive quantity.

It is difficult to give the third reason concisely and clearly, as St Thomas touches on a deep question in philosophy: 'What is the principle of individuation?'

His argument may be illustrated thus: If a single sheet of paper is divided into four unequal parts, there are four similar substances. For substance can be divided on account of quantity, as is said in Phys. I, and therefore dimensive quantity itself is a particular principle of individuation.

For every one of these four pieces is quantitatively distinct from every other.

What gives each individual existence? The fact that dimensive quantity (or area) of the paper is capable of being divided. These pieces can be sub-divided until the area or dimensive quantity is so small as to be incapable of further division. And yet *all* the accidents of paper would naturally remain with the substance within the area of the tiniest piece *and none* of them outside of it. Hence St Thomas concludes: Dimensive quantity can be the subject of the other accidents and not the other way about. (cf. English *Summa*, Part III, QQ. 60-83, pp. 310-11. See also Appendix V on p. 177 of the present work.)

Obj. I. An accident is not the subject of an accident. But dimensive quantity is an accident; therefore it cannot be the subject of other accidents.

Reply. When God makes an accident to exist of itself, it can also be of itself the subject of other accidents.

Obj. II. Substance individuates other accidents as well as quantity. If the dimensive quantity of the bread and wine remain individuated after consecration according to the mode of being it had before, so also should all the other accidents.

Reply. They were individuated by means of dimensive quantity before consecration; therefore dimensive quantity remains the subject after as well as before.

Obj. III. Rarity and density remain; but they cannot be in dimensive quantity existing outside matter; for a thing is rare which has little matter under great dimension and dense which has much matter under small dimensions.

Reply. As the accidents are preserved by divine power when the substance is withdrawn, so also those qualities which go with matter such as rarity and density.

Obj. IV. Quantity separated from its subject seems to

be mathematical quantity.[1] But mathematical quantity is not the subject of sensible qualities. Therefore since the accidents which remain in this sacrament are sensible, it seems they cannot exist there as in a subject, in the dimensive quantity of the bread and wine after consecration.

Reply. Mathematical quantity does not abstract[2] from intelligible matter,[3] but from sensible matter (cf. *Metaph*, L. 7, Text 35). But matter is said to be sensible because it underlies sensible qualities; therefore it is clear that the dimensive quantity which remains in this sacrament without a subject is not mathematical but physical quantity.

Can the species that remain change anything external to them?

(Q. 77, 3)

Yes. If they cannot alter exterior bodies their presence cannot be felt.

By divine power the sacramental species continue in the *being* they had when the substance of the bread and wine was present. Therefore they continue in their *action*. For everything acts in so far as it is in actual being.

Obj. I. The sacramental species exist without matter; therefore they cannot affect other matter.

---

1 Mathematical quantity is an abstraction from sensible matter (i.e., that which falls under the senses), and hence is considered as purely intelligible. It is simply magnitude, *or the want of it.* For instance, we speak of a point, a line, a surface. A point has neither length, breadth nor thickness, and therefore has not magnitude. A line has length, but no breadth or depth. A surface has length and breadth but no thickness.

2 Abstraction (*abs* from, *trahere* to draw) is that act of the intellect which disengages or considers apart some peculiar and individual element of a material body (even though it exists with other elements in their material setting. For example *cold* in ice, *hardness* in diamonds).

Abstraction is a single instantaneous act. This act of the intellect is likened to the sun illuminating colours indiscernible in darkness, and the intellect itself is compared to the artist who turns towards the object he is about to copy (cf. Maher's *Psychology*, p. 296).

3 Intelligible matter is so called because perceived by the intellect, and only affects the senses by mere accident (cf. note I, 85, ad 2), as a line, surface, etc.

Reply. They still retain the same being they had before in matter.

Obj. II. When the principle agent, viz., the substance of the bread and wine does not remain, it would seem that the accidental forms cannot act upon or change external matter. Just as when the carpenter rests the hammer moves no more.

Reply. As the sacramental species *exist* without substance by divine power so they can also *act* without a substantial form; for every action of a form, be it substantial or accidental, depends on *God as the First Agent.* (Therefore even when the carpenter rests, the hammer can continue to act by divine power.)

Obj. III. Sacramental species are accidents. They cannot then alter external matter, at least as regards its substantial form, otherwise the effect is greater than its cause.

Reply. By divine power the species can affect substantial forms *instrumentally.*

(An example would be: heat changes wood into charcoal. Heat is an accident; and by divine power the heat can continue to do so, even when the fire is removed.)

Can the Sacramental Species be corrupted? (Q. 77, 4)

Yes. Our senses prove they can. Since they retain the same being they had when the substance of the bread was present and could then have been corrupted so also when the substance passed away.

The accidents can be corrupted in two ways: (*a*) of themselves, or (*b*) accidentally. First of themselves by alteration of the quality or increase or decrease of quantity; for the dimensive quantity which is the subject of all other sensible qualities can also be the subject of their alteration; secondly, accidentally, by a contrary agent: but a distinction must be made between them.

If the change on the part of the accidents would not

corrupt the bread and wine, then the body and blood of Christ which succeed them, do not cease to be, when for instance the colour or taste of the bread or wine is slightly altered, or when the bread or wine is divided into such parts as still to retain the nature of bread and wine.

But if the change be so great that the substance of bread and wine would have been corrupted, then Christ's body and blood do not remain. This change may be either in the quality, when the colour, taste and other qualities are no longer consistent with the nature of bread and wine, or when the appearances of the bread are reduced to powder or of the wine to such very small drops that the species no longer remain.

Obj. I. Corruption comes from the separation of matter and form. But the matter of the bread does not remain, therefore the species cannot be corrupted.

Obj. II. Self-subsisting forms are incorruptible, as is seen in spiritual substances (the angels). But the sacramental species are forms without a subject; therefore they cannot be corrupted.

Reply. The answer to the second objection also meets the first, viz., that although the sacramental species are not forms in matter yet they have the *being* they had in matter.

Obj. III. If the species were corrupted, it would either be naturally or miraculously. It cannot occur naturally: for suppose such a corruption to have run its course, it is impossible to assign any corruptible thing in which it can have occurred; nor can such a hypothetical corruption take place miraculously; for the miracles wrought in this sacrament are wrought in virtue of consecration; now the miracle wrought here is the miracle of conserving the sacramental appearances apart from their substance, but the same cause cannot produce conservation and corruption, its opposite.

Reply. The corruption of the species is natural, not miraculous; but it presupposes the miracle wrought in consecration, whereby these species retain the same being without a subject as they had in a subject, just as a blind man, miraculously cured, sees naturally.

Can anything be generated from the Sacramental Species?
(Q. 77, 5)

Yes. The senses testify that ashes are generated out of them if burned, dust if they are crushed, worms if they putrefy[1] (by the action of larvae).

Since the species do not disappear entirely, something must be generated from them if corrupted; for evidently something sensible succeeds them. But the difficulty is, how? For nothing can be generated out of the body and blood of Christ which are truly there; because these are incorruptible. If the substance or even the matter of the bread and wine remained, it would be easy to explain the change; but the underlying supposition is false (cf. Q. 75, 2, 4, 8).

Others say that what is generated does not spring from the sacramental species but from the surrounding atmosphere. This is impossible.

First, because when one thing is generated from another that other must first appear changed or corrupted; but there is no change in the surrounding atmosphere; secondly, the nature of air does not permit such a kind of generation.

Others hold that the substance of the bread and wine returns during the corruption of the species; and from it ashes, etc., are generated.

---

1 Worms cannot be generated *from* the sacramental species but *on* them, viz., by insects depositing their larvae upon them, which in turn, feed on the sacramental species and change and corrupt them.

This explanation also is impossible: first, because the body and blood cannot be changed back into either substance, no more than air if changed into fire can return without fire being also changed into air.

Again, if the substance of the bread and wine be annihilated, it cannot return,[1] because what is reduced to nothing does not return numerically the same. But some one may say that the substance of the bread and wine returns because God creates another new substance to replace the first. This seems impossible, because no one can say when the substance of bread returns.

It is not (a) while the species of the bread and wine remain; for then only the body and blood of Christ can be present as said above (75, 2). Nor again (b) when the species pass away; because the substance of the bread and wine would be without their proper accidents which cannot be.[2] So it seems better to say that in the actual consecration a miraculous power is bestowed on the dimensive quantity of the bread and wine to become the subject of subsequent forms. Therefore anything which could be generated from the matter of bread and wine, if it were present, can be generated from the dimensive quantity of bread and wine, not by a new miracle but by virtue of the miracle that had already taken place.

Obj. I. There is no matter beneath the sacramental species unless that of Christ's body; and it is incorruptible: therefore it seems nothing can be generated from the sacramental species.

Reply. Dimensive quantity takes the place of matter, as said above.

Obj. II. Things not of the same genus cannot spring

---

1 Apart from a miracle, for God can by his absolute power reproduce numerically the same matter that has been annihilated.
2 The only possible way is if the matter of the bread and wine returns, which St Thomas says should be said rather to be created anew than returning.

from one another. A line for instance is not made from whiteness; but accident and substance differ generically. Therefore since the sacramental species are accidents, no substance can be generated from them.

Reply. The sacramental species are of course accidents; but they have the act and power of substance (cf. 77, 1 and 4).

Obj. III. It is impossible for substance and accidents to be generated from accidents only.

Reply. The dimensive quantity of the bread and wine retains miraculously the power and property of substance and therefore can pass to both; that is, to substance and dimension.

Can the Sacramental Species nourish? (Q. 77, 6)

Yes. The apostle says: '*One indeed is hungry and another is drunk.*' (1 Cor. 11, 21.) That is, according to the gloss, he reproves those who after the consecration of the bread and wine claimed their oblations, gave nothing to others but took the whole, and thus became intoxicated. This could not happen if the sacramental species did not nourish by being converted into the substance of the recipient. When the sacramental species can turn into ashes and worms, for the same reason they can be converted into the human body and certainly nourish it.

Our senses tell us that it is not true to say that the species do not nourish by being changed into the human body but merely refresh and strengthen it, just like a man being stimulated by the odour of meat and intoxicated by the fumes of wine.

For such refreshment does not suffice long for a man; but he could live for a long time if he were to take Hosts and consecrated wine in great quantity.

Again it does not hold what others maintain, that the sacramental species nourish because the substantial form of the bread and wine remain. As said above in Q. 76, 6, the form does not remain; and to nourish is the act of the matter, not of the form. Matter takes the *form* of the person nourished, while the form of the nourishment passes away. Hence it is said of nourishment that at first it is unlike and at the end is like (*De Anima* 2).

Obj. I. St Ambrose says: 'It is not this bread which enters into our body, but the bread of eternal life which supports the substance of the soul.' But whatever nourishes enters the body; therefore this bread or the species of the wine does not nourish.

Reply. Christ's own body can be called bread since it is the mystical bread coming from Heaven. So when St Ambrose says 'This bread does not pass into the body' he means that Christ's body is not changed into man's body but nourishes the soul. In other words the substance of Christ's body nourishes the soul and the accidents that remain of the bread nourish the body.

Obj. II. We are nourished by the very things of which we are made. The species are accidents. But man is not made of accidents; therefore the species cannot nourish.

Reply. When the sacramental species can be changed into dust they can also be changed into the human body, which was formed from it.

Obj. III. 'Food nourishes according as it is a substance, but gives increase by reason of its quantity.' Now the sacramental species are not a substance therefore they cannot nourish.

Reply. Although not a substance, the species have the virtue of a substance as said above.

Are the Sacramental Species broken? (Q. 77, 7)

Yes. Breaking is due to quantity being divided.

But in this sacrament nothing having quantity except the species is broken. Neither Christ's body is broken since incorruptible, nor the substance of the bread since it does not remain.

Some used to hold that there was really no breaking but that it was merely in the eyes of the beholders. This is not so; for in this sacrament of truth, sense cannot be deceived in its proper objects of judgment: and one of these is breaking by which one thing becomes many, and these are common sensibles[1] (namely, those which can be perceived by several senses).

Some held that there was a real breaking but without a subject. This also contradicts our senses; for a quantitative body is seen which had been one and now is many; and this must be the subject of the breaking.

But Christ's body is not broken since incorruptible, impassible and entire in every part. Dimensive quantity is therefore the subject of this breaking just as it is the subject of the other accidents.

Obj. I. Breakableness is due to a certain disposition of the pores: this cannot be attributed to the sacred species. Therefore they cannot be broken.

Reply. Porosity remains just as rarity and density do; so also breakableness.

Obj. III. Berengarius confessed: 'The bread and wine placed on the altar are the true body and blood of Christ after consecration, and are truly broken by the priest's hands and crushed by the teeth of the believers.' Therefore the breaking is not to be ascribed to the sacred species.

Reply. What is eaten under its own species is also broken: but Christ's body is eaten not under its proper but its sacramental species. Hence St Augustine explains the words: '*The flesh profiteth nothing*' (John 7, 64).

---

1 Proper sensibles only appeal to our particular senses: colour to the eye, sound to the ear.

'They (the Jews) understood the flesh as divided in a dead body or as sold in the shambles.'

So Christ's body is not broken except according to its sacramental species; and it is to them that Berengarius's confession refers.

Can any liquid be mingled wtih the Consecrated Wine?
(Q. 77, 8)

Yes. This is evident to our senses; for just as the species acquire the *being* of substance in virtue of the consecration: so they also acquire the mode of *acting* and of being acted upon, and therefore they can receive whatever the substance receives if it were present.

The effect of mixing varies according to the form and quantity of the liquor. If it suffices to spread all through the wine, there is a mixed or third substance; and the former substance would remain no longer whether the liquid added be the same or of a different species.

Hence if water were added in a large quantity, the species of the wine would be dissolved and there would be a liquid of another species; or if wine were added the same species would remain; but the wine would not be numerically the same; for instance if one wine were red and the other white.

But if so little liquid were added as not to spread through the whole, it would be the same specifically, even if it were a different species, since a drop of water would pass into the species of the wine.

Now since it is *this* bread and *this* wine which is consecrated, the body and blood of Christ remain as long as the species are numerically the same. Hence if any kind of liquid be so added as to mix with all the consecrated wine, the result is something numerically distinct; and the blood of Christ will remain there no longer. If the quantity added only mixes with a part of the species, Christ's blood ceases to be under that part and remains under the rest.

Obj. I. No liquid can share in the quality of the sacramental species; because these accidents are without a subject.

Reply. Innocent III writes: 'Accidents change the subject just as subject changes accident; for nature yields to miracle and power works beyond custom.' This does not mean that the self-same accidents in the wine *before* consecration are *afterwards* in the wine that is added: but such a change is due to the action of the accidents of the consecrated wine retaining the action of substance.

Obj. II. If any liquor be mixed with the species then from these one thing must result. But nothing can result from the liquid which is a substance, and the sacred species which are accidents, or from the liquid and the blood of Christ which is incorruptible and cannot increase or decrease.

Reply. The liquid in no way mixes with the substance of Christ's blood, but with the sacred species which are corrupted either entirely, or in part. If entirely, no further question remains because the whole will be uniform. (And Christ's blood ceases to be there.)

If in part there will be one dimension according to continuity of quantity, but not one according to the mode of being; just as in a body made up of two metals, quantitively, there is one body, but not one as to the species of the matter.

Obj. III. Water added to holy water becomes holy, therefore the liquid added to consecrated wine is Christ's blood without being consecrate, which is unbecoming.

Reply. It is not the same with holy water; for the blessing makes no change in the substance of the water as the consecration of the wine does.

Obj. IV. White and black cause a difference of colour; so liquid mixed, be it little or much, would corrupt the entire species of the sacramental wine present.

Reply. More or less diversify quantity, not as to its essence but as to the determination of its measure. (Liquid added can be so small as not to permeate the whole, just as very little white or black would not perceptibly change the colour.)

CHAPTER VI

THE FORM OF
THE BLESSED SACRAMENT

Is the form: 'This is My Body' and 'This is the Chalice of My Blood'? (Q. 78, 1)

YES. St Ambrose says 'The consecration is accomplished by the words of the Lord Jesus: when the time comes for perfecting the venerable sacrament, the priest no longer uses his own words but the words of Christ.'

This sacrament differs from the rest in two ways.

First, it is accomplished by the consecration of the matter. The others are perfected by the use of consecrated matter.

Secondly, in them the consecration of the matter consists only in a blessing and confers instrumentally a spiritual power which can pass through a priest to inanimate instruments. But in the Eucharist the consecration of the matter consists in the miraculous change of the substance, due to God alone.

Hence all the minister does in this sacrament is to pronounce the words; and as the form should suit the words it differs in this sacrament from the others in two ways.

First, the latter imply the *use* of matter as for instance, baptizing, anointing. The former merely implies the *consecration* of the matter which consists in transubstantiation, as when it is said: '*This is my body.*'

Secondly, the forms of the other sacraments are pronounced in the person of the minister, whether by act, by entreaty, or by command: as 'I baptize thee'. 'By this holy unction', or in holy orders 'Take the power', etc.

But the form of this sacrament is pronounced as if Christ were speaking in person—so the minister does nothing to perfect this sacrament but pronounce the words of Christ.

Obj. I. Christ first blessed the bread and then said '*Take ye and eat—This is my body.*' Therefore the whole of this seems to belong to the form of this sacrament; and the same applies to the consecration of the blood.

Reply. There are many opinions of the subject: Some held that Christ who had the power of excellence used no words, but afterwards pronounced the words whereby others were to consecrate; as for instance Innocent III said: 'Christ accomplished this sacrament by his divine power and then expressed the form.' But the gospel says Christ *blessed*; and this blessing was effected by certain words: so these words of Innocent III rather express an opinion than determine the point.

Others again hold that the blessing was effected by different words not known to us. This cannot stand; for if the consecration was not performed then by these words, neither would it be now.

Others hold that Christ spoke the words of consecration twice: first, secretly to *consecrate*, and secondly openly to *instruct*. This will not stand either; for since these words have no power except from Christ pronouncing them: it seems that Christ consecrated by uttering them openly as the priest does now.

Others held that the evangelists did not always follow the exact order (cf. Augustine. *De Consensu Evang.* II.). Hence it may be expressed thus: *Taking the bread he blessed it saying 'This is my body.' And then he broke it and gave to his disciples.*

But the same can be said even without changing the

words of the Gospel; because the participle *saying* implies sequence and can be understood with regard to all that had gone before; so that the meaning is: while he was blessing and breaking and giving it to his disciples he spoke the words, 'Take ye', etc.

Obj. II. Eusebius of Emesa says, 'The invisible priest changes visible creatures into his own body, saying: *Take ye and eat. This is my body.* Therefore the whole of this seems to belong to the form.

Reply. In these words (*Take ye and eat*) the *use* is indicated which is not of the necessity of this sacrament, as said above (Q. 74, 7). Therefore, even the words '*Take ye and eat*' do not belong to the substance of the form. Still, as the *use* belongs to a certain perfection of the sacrament in the same way as operation is not the first but the second perfection of a thing, therefore the *whole* perfection of this sacrament is expressed by all these words; and it is thus Eusebius is to be understood.

Obj. III. In the form of Baptism the words 'I baptize thee' express both the minister and his act. But there is no mention of either in the words 'This is my body', therefore this form is not suitable.

Reply. In Baptism the act of the minister regarding the *use* of matter is of the essence of sacrament. (It is not so in this sacrament, for the words are those of Christ himself and they convert the matter into Christ's body which is then present for the *use* of the priest and of the faithful.)

Obj. IV. One can baptize by pronouncing the words of the form only, omitting all others, therefore one should also be able to consecrate this sacrament by uttering the words only and leaving out all others.

Reply. Some held that this sacrament cannot be consecrated by pronouncing the aforesaid words whilst leaving out the rest, especially the Canon of the Mass. But this

is false as we may see from the words of St Ambrose:
'The consecration is accomplished by the words of the
Lord Jesus; because by all others spoken, praise is given to
God, prayer is offered for the people. When the time
comes for the perfecting of this sacrament, the priest no
longer uses his own words.' And again the Canon of the
Mass is not the same everywhere (testifying to the uni-
versal tradition against using the form alone).

Were the priest to pronounce the form of this sacrament, it would be valid; because the intention would
make it clearly understood that these words were spoken
in the person of Christ. The priest however would sin
gravely by consecrating in this way; and no comparison
with baptism could be urged; as it is a sacrament of
necessity, whereas the want of this sacrament can be sup-
plied by the spiritual partaking thereof. (cf. Q. 73, 3 ad 1.)

*Is 'This is My Body' the proper form for the Consecration of
the Bread?* (Q. 78, 2)

Yes. The form ought to signify what is done in the
sacrament, namely, the actual conversion of the bread
into the body of Christ.

Three things are to be considered: the conversion itself,
and the terms *whence* (that from which) and *whereunto*
(that into which).

The conversion can be considered in two ways: in *becoming (in fieri)* and in *being (in facto esse)*. But in this form
conversion ought not to be considered as in *becoming* but
as in *being*. First, because the change is not successive but
instantaneous; and therefore the *becoming* is nothing else
but the *being*. Secondly, because the form of a sacrament
is calculated to express the effect of the sacrament in much
the same way as the plan of the house constructed precedes in the builder's mind its actual construction.

And because in the form (of the Blessed Sacrament) the

conversion is expressed as *in being*, hence it is necessary that the extreme points of the conversion (namely, *that from which* and *that into which*) be expressed as they are when the conversion is completed. But at that point '*that into which*' has the proper nature of its own substance, whereas *that from which* no longer remains according to its native substance but only according to its accidents.

Hence the term *whence* may be expressed by the demonstrative pronoun *relatively* to the sensible accidents which remain, whilst the term *whereunto* is expressed by the noun denoting the nature of the thing terminating the conversion; that is, Christ's entire body and not merely his flesh as said above (76, Art. 1 ad 2). Hence, 'This is my body' is the most appropriate form.

Obj. I. The effect of a sacrament ought to be expressed in its form. But the effect of the consecration of the bread is better expressed by the word 'become' than by 'is'.

Reply. The last effect of this conversion is not a *becoming* but a *being*, as said above; therefore this should be emphasized in the form.

Obj. II. St Ambrose says 'Christ's words consecrate this sacrament. What word of Christ's? The word by which all things are made.' Therefore it would be better to use the imperative mood in the form and say: '*Be this my body.*'

Reply. God's word operates in creation, and in the consecration; yet in each in a different way; in creation *merely effectively*, in consecration *effectively* and *sacramentally*; that is by virtue of its signification. Then the last effect of consecration must be signified by a verb in the indicative mood, present tense. Whilst in creation wherein God works merely effectively, such efficiency is due to the *command* of his wisdom and therefore is expressed by the imperative mood as: 'Let there be light, and light was made.' (Gen. I, 3.)

Obj. III. When the predicate is something determinate, so also should the subject. Therefore the form should be: '*This bread is my body.*'

Reply. The term *whence* (i.e. the bread) does not retain the nature of its substance in the *being*[1] of the conversion as the term *whereunto* does, therefore there is no parallel.

Obj. IV. As the term of conversion is determinate in nature; because it is a body; so also it is determinate in person; consequently, to determine the person, it ought to be said: '*This is THE body of Christ.*'

Reply. The pronoun *my* implies the chief person.

Obj. V. The conjunction 'for' is improperly added, since it does not belong to the substance of the form.

Reply. It is added according to the custom of the Roman Church, who derived it from Peter, the Apostle; and this, on account of the sequence with the preceding words; and therefore it is not a part of the form any more than the words that precede it.

Is this the proper form for the Consecration of the Wine: '*This is the Chalice of my Blood of the New and Eternal Testament, the Mystery of Faith which for you and for many will be shed for the remission of sins*'*?* (Q. 78, 3)

Yes. The Church instructed by the Apostles uses this form.

Some hold that only the words: '*This is the chalice of my blood*' belong to the substance of this form but not those which follow. This seems incorrect as the words which do follow determine the predicate; that is, Christ's blood. Hence they belong to the integrity of these solemn

---

1 'Being' here means the change of substance: ' whereunto' the body of Christ. St Thomas's words are: 'Terminus *a quo* in ipso *facto esse* conversionis non retinet naturam suae substantiae sicut terminus *ad quem*.'

words. So others say more correctly that all are of the substance of the form which follow as far as the words: '*As often as ye shall do this*', which belong to the *use* of the sacrament, not to the substance of the form.

Hence the priest in pronouncing these words still holds the chalice in his hands.

As regards those that belong to the substance of the form, the change of the wine into blood is denoted by the words: '*This is the chalice of my blood.*' But St Luke says (12, 20) '*This is the chalice. The New Testament in my blood which shall be shed for you.*' Here the words that precede are interposed with those that follow. Therefore it must be said that all the aforesaid words '*This is the chalice of my blood of the New and Eternal Testament which for you and for many will be shed for the remission of sins*' belong to the substance of the form.

But by the first words '*This is the chalice of my blood*' the actual conversion of wine into blood is denoted. The words which follow, '*The New and Eternal Testament*', show the power of the blood shed in the Passion which works in this sacrament, and is ordained for three ends:

First and principally, to secure our eternal inheritance according to Heb .10, 19: '*Having confidence in the entering into the holies by the blood of Christ.*'

Secondly to justify grace by, which is by *faith* according to Rom. 3, 25, 26: '*Whom God hath proposed to be a propitiation through faith in his blood that he himself may be just and the justifier of him who is of the faith of Jesus Christ.*' And on this account we add '*The mystery of faith.*'

Thirdly, to remove sins so opposed to both these things according to Heb. 9, 19. '*The blood of Christ shall cleanse our conscience from dead works*', that is from sins; and for this reason we say: '*Which shall be shed for you and for many unto the remission of sins.*'

Obj. I. It seems this form: '*This is the chalice of my blood*, etc.', is not correct, for in that of the consecration of the bread, '*This is my body*', the word *body* is in the direct or nominative case and nothing more is added; but in this form the blood of Christ is improperly in an oblique case and the chalice in the nominative, when it is said: '*This is the chalice of my blood.*'

Reply. First, this may be taken as a figure of metonomy (or the container for the contained), so that the meaning is: '*This is my blood contained in the chalice.*' This blood is the *drink* of the faithful. But blood is not regarded as a beverage; so it has to be denoted by a vessel adapted for such use. Secondly, these words may be taken metaphorically, so that the chalice may be compared to Christ's Passion; because like a cup it inebriates, according to Lam. 3, 13: '*He hath filled me with bitterness, he hath inebriated me with wormwood.*' Hence our Lord spoke of his Passion as a chalice: '*Let this chalice pass from me*' (Matt. 26, 39). Then the meaning is: '*This is the chalice of my Passion*', and that is denoted by the blood being consecrated apart from the body: because, by the Passion, the blood was separated from the body.

Obj. II. There is a perfect consecration of the bread the moment the words are spoken '*This is my body*'; and again, when the words '*This is the chalice of my blood*' are uttered, there is a perfect consecration of the blood; so the words which follow do not seem to belong to the substance of the form.

Reply. The fruits of the Passion are mentioned in the consecration of the blood rather than in that of the body, since it (the body) is the subject of the Passion: our Lord meant this when he said: '*which shall be delivered up for you*', that is, *which shall undergo the Passion for you.*

Obj. III. The New Testament seems to be an internal

inspiration according to St Paul, Heb. 8, 10, quoting Jeremias (31, 33) '*I will give my laws unto their minds.*' But a sacrament is an external visible act; therefore in this form the words 'of the New Testament' are improperly added.

Reply. Christ's blood was exhibited in two ways: in the Old Testament in figure, in the New Testament in very truth. Therefore we say here: '*The blood of the New Testament*', because it is shown now, not in figure but in very truth; and therefore we add '*which shall be shed for you*'. But the internal inspiration arises from the power of the blood according as we are justified by Christ's Passion.

Obj. IV. What is eternal has no beginning, therefore it is incorrect to say '*of the New and Eternal*' for a thing is new which *begins* to exist.

Reply. This Testament is new in the way it shows forth (God's love) and yet it is called *eternal* on account of the eternal inheritance prepared by this Testament; and again Christ's Person is eternal in whose blood this Testament is appointed.

Obj. V. Isaias says: '*Take away the stumbling blocks out of the way of my people*' (57, 14). But some have erred by thinking that Christ's body and blood are only mystically in this sacrament; therefore the words '*the mystery of faith*' should not be added.

Reply. The word 'mystery' is inserted not to exclude reality, but to show that the reality is hidden; because Christ's blood is in this sacrament in a hidden way.

Obj. VI. St Paul says, '*As often as you shall eat of this bread and drink of this chalice you shall show the death of the Lord*' (1 Cor. 11, 26). Therefore Christ's Passion and its fruit should be mentioned in the form of the consecration of the blood rather than in that of the consecration of the body.

Reply. The evangelists did not intend to hand down the forms of the sacraments, which in the primitive Church had to be concealed. Their object was to write the history of Christ; but all these words can be gathered from various passages of the Gospels. The words added, *eternal* and *mystery of faith*, were handed down to the Church by the apostles who received them from our Lord according to 1 Cor. 11, 23 : '*I have received of the Lord that which also I have delivered unto you.*'

Is there any created power in the aforesaid words which causes the Consecration? (Q. 78, 4)

Yes. St Ambrose says: 'If such is the power in the word of the Lord Jesus that what was not, begins to be: how much more can it make what is, not only to remain but also to change into something else; and so what was bread before consecration is now the body of Christ after consecration, because Christ's word changes a creature into something different.'

To say no, is contrary to the teachings of the saints and detracts from the dignity of the sacraments of the New Law (cf. Q. 72, 1.).

Hence, since this sacrament surpasses the rest (Q. 65, 3), there is in the words of the form a created power which effects the change, but instrumental as in the other sacraments (Q. 62, 1, 3, 4); for since these words are pronounced in the person of Christ, it is from his command they derive their instrumental power.

Obj. 1. St John Damascene says 'The change of the bread into Christ's body is caused solely by the power of the Holy Ghost.' But that power is increased; therefore this sacrament is not caused by any created power of those words.

Reply. The instrumental power which is in the form of this sacrament is not excluded, just as when we say

F

'the smith alone makes a knife' the power of the hammer
is not denied.

Obj. II. The change of the bread and wine into Christ's
body and blood is a work not less miraculous than creation, or the formation of Christ's body in the Virgin's
womb; but of these neither could be done by any created
power.

Reply. No creature can work miracles as the *chief
agent*; but it can instrumentally. Just as the touch of
Christ's hand healed the leper, so Christ's word changed
the bread into his body; but in his conception, it was
impossible for anything derived from his body to have
the instrumental power of forming that selfsame body.
And in creation there was no extreme wherein the instrumental action of a creature could be received. So there is
no comparison. (For instance, anyone could change ice
into steam, two extremes, but no one, save God, could
change nothingness into something.)

Obj. III. The words of this form are not simple but
many and not pronounced simultaneously but successively. . . . But as said above (75, 7) this change is instantaneous; hence, it must be done by a simple power, and
therefore not by the power of the words of the form.

Reply. These words work *sacramentally*; therefore the
converting power underlying their forms follows the
meaning which terminates in the last word uttered; and
the power they have then is taken in conjunction with the
words uttered before. This power is simple by reason of
the thing signified although outwardly there is a kind of
composition in the words uttered.

*Are the aforesaid expressions true: 'This is my Body'—
'This is the Chalice of my Blood'?* (Q. 78, 5)

Yes. These words are pronounced in the person of
Christ, who says of himself '*I am the Truth*' (John 14, 6),

First. Some held that the word *This* in the form 'This is my body' means that the priest merely relates that Christ said: '*This is my body*' and therefore the word *This* implies demonstrations as conceived and not as exercised.

The words then would not be *applied* to the matter present: and there would be no sacrament; for St Augustine says: 'The word is added to the element and it becomes a sacrament.'

Again, when Christ first pronounced these words, he did not merely recite them, but *effected* what they signified: that is, he used them *significatively*; and so does every priest, even though he utters them by way of recital, as though they were spoken by Christ. Because owing to Christ's infinite power, just as by contact with his flesh the regenerative power entered not only into these waters which touched Christ, but into all the waters in the whole world, and during all future ages. So also from the fact of Christ uttering these words himself, they derive their consecrating power by whatever priest they may be pronounced, as if Christ present were saying them.

Second. Again, others said that the word *This* appeals to the intellect, not to the senses, so that the meaning is: The thing *signified* by 'This' is my body. But a sacrament does not merely signify; it *effects* what it signifies. Therefore from such a form it would follow that Christ's body was not in very truth in this sacrament, but merely in a sign, which is heretical as said above (75, 1).

Third. Others then said that the word *This* appeals to the senses, not at the exact moment it is spoken, but only at the very last instant of the sentence, as when someone says 'Now, I am silent'. This adverb *Now* points to the instant *following* the last word spoken; for the meaning is 'once these words are said, I am silent'. From this explanation it would follow that the form means 'This body is my body', and would not effect what it signifies; because the body was not there before the words were spoken at all.

It only remains to be said as above (Art. 4) that this form has the *effective* power of changing bread into the body of Christ.

Therefore these words are to other phrases that only signify and do not produce, what the practical intellect, which does produce, is to the speculative which does not; and whose concepts are derived from (exterior) objects: 'For words are signs of concepts.'

Therefore, as the concept of the practical intellect does not presuppose the thing conceived, but makes it, so the truth of these solemn words does not presuppose the thing signified, but makes it; for such is the word of God to the things made by the word.

Now this conversion is not successive but instantaneous, as said above (75, 7). Therefore the words of the form must refer to the last instant they are spoken; yet not in such a way that the *subject* of the conversion is the *term* of conversion; that is, that the body of Christ is the body of Christ.

Nor again, that it is what it was before conversion, namely bread; but what is contained in general under these species is common to both.

For these words do not make the body of Christ to be the body of Christ nor the bread to be the body of Christ, *but what was contained under those species, and formerly bread, they make to be the body of Christ.*

And therefore our Lord does not expressly say: '*This bread is my body*', nor 'This my body is my body', but in general 'This —— is my body', assigning no noun on the part of the subject, but only a pronoun, which signifies substance in common, *without quality*; that is without a determinate form.

Obj. I. The word *This* in the form 'This is my body' points to a substance. But it was said (Art. 2) that when the pronoun *This* is spoken, the substance of the bread is still there: for transubstantiation only occurs the instant the last word is pronounced.

Reply. The term *This* points to a substance but does not determine its proper nature.

Obj. II. The pronoun *This* appeals to the senses. But the sensible species in this sacrament are neither Christ's body nor its accidents. Therefore these words: '*This is my body*' cannot be true.

Reply. The pronoun *This* does not point to these accidents, but to the body of Christ, which although not informed by these accidents is contained under them.

Obj. III. The words of the form '*This is my body*' effect what they signify, namely, the conversion of bread into the body of Christ; and a cause should precede its effect. But previous to the change, that is, before the last word was pronounced, it was false to say: '*This is my body*'; therefore the form is to be judged simply as false and likewise the words '*This is the chalice of my blood.*'

Reply. In the order of *nature* the cause comes before the effect. But in the order of *time* this is not so; as both go together at one and the same instant. (Therefore the form must be true; for it has no specific meaning until the last essential word is pronounced; and at the same instant the conversion takes place.)

Does the form of the Consecration of the Bread obtain its effects before the form of the Consecration of the Wine is completed?
(Q. 78, 6)

Yes. For once the words of consecration are spoken, the host is shown to the people to be adored; and if

Christ's body was not there, it would be an act of idolatry.

Some ancient doctors thought that the first form did not produce its effect until the second was pronounced.

This is not so; because as said above (78, 3 and 5) the verb must be in the present tense; for the thing signified by the form, '*This is my body*', must be present at the same time as the signifying expression is used; otherwise if the body is not present, but yet to come, a verb of the future and not the present tense should be used; and therefore we should *not say* 'This *is* my body' but 'This *will be* my body.'

Now what the words signify is complete the instant they are spoken; therefore the things signified must also be instantly present; for such is the effect of the sacrament; otherwise it would not be a true expression.

Obj. I. If the words for the consecration of the bread produce their effect before the consecration of the wine, it would follow that Christ's body is present without the blood, which is improper.

Reply. As stated above (76, 2) once the consecration of the bread is complete, the body of Christ is present by the power of the sacrament and the blood by real concomitance.

Obj. II. There are three immersions in Baptism, yet the first does not produce its effect until the third is completed. But all this sacrament is one as said above (73, 2); therefore the words by which the bread is consecrated do not produce their effect without the sacramental words by which the wine is consecrated.

Reply. The three immersions in Baptism are ordained to one simple effect; but this sacrament is one in perfection, being made up of food and drink, each of which has its own perfection: so there is no parallel.

Obj. III. The words of consecration are many and do not produce their effect until the last word is pronounced. For the same reason, the words of consecration of Christ's body cannot produce their effect until the words are pronounced by which Christ's blood is consecrated.

Reply. There is no parity. The words of the form for the consecration of the bread constitute the truth of *one* speech. But the words of the *different* forms do not.

CHAPTER VII

THE EFFECTS OF THIS SACRAMENT

Is Grace conferred through this Sacrament? (Q. 79, 1)
YES. Our Lord says, '*The bread which I will give is my flesh for the life of the world*' (John 6, 52).

But spiritual life is due to grace, therefore it is given by this sacrament for four reasons:

First, and above all, what is contained in it is Christ himself. And just as he bestowed the life of grace on the world by coming visibly into it, for '*Grace and truth come by Jesus Christ*' (John 1, 17), so also by coming sacramentally he produces the life of grace in man according to the words: '*He that eateth me, the same shall live by me*' (John 6, 58).

Hence St Cyril says: 'It was becoming that he (Christ) should be united in some way with our bodies through his sacred flesh and precious blood which we receive (under the appearances of) bread and wine, unto a life-giving blessing.'

Secondly, because Christ's Passion is re-presented by this sacrament, as said above (74, 1; 76 2 ad 1). Therefore it produces in each individual man the effect wrought by Christ's Passion on the world at large. Hence St Chrysostom commenting on the words of St John: 'Immediately there came out blood and water', exclaims 'When you draw nigh to the chalice, approach with awe and as if you were to drink from Christ's own side', and hence too, our Lord says himself, '*This is my blood which shall be shed for many for the remission of sins*' (Matt. 26, 28).

Third, because this sacrament does for the spiritual life all that material food does for the bodily life, namely, sustaining, giving increase, restoring and giving pleasure. Therefore St Ambrose says, 'That bread is rightly called the bread of life which props up and sustains the very substance of the soul'; and St Chrysostom declares, '*When we wish it, he lets us feel him and eat him and embrace him.*' Hence our Lord says, '*My flesh is meat indeed: my blood is drink indeed*' (John 6, 56).

Fourthly, because of the species under which this sacrament is bestowed: for St Augustine says: 'Our Lord left us his body and blood in the guise of those things which are made into one whole out of many units (as for instance bread from many grains and wine from many grapes); and therefore he exclaims elsewhere: 'O, sacrament of tenderness', 'O, sign of unity', 'O, bond of charity'.

Now, since Christ and his Passion are the cause of grace, and there is neither spiritual refreshment nor charity without grace, evidently this sacrament confers it.

Obj. I. How can grace be conferred in this sacrament in any way at all? It cannot give first grace, that is change one in mortal sin to the state of grace; for apparently it is the sacrament of spiritual nourishment; and nourishment only benefits the living. Neither can it give an increase of grace to one already in the state of grace, for, as said above to give an increase of sanctifying grace belongs to Confirmation (72, I).

Reply. So true is it that this sacrament confers sanctifying grace that no one has any grace at all except by virtue of a desire of receiving this sacrament. If an adult, the desire must be personal. If a child the desire must be had in the Church. Hence the efficacy of the sacrament is such that even through its very desire man receives grace by which he is made to live spiritually. (That is, he shares in the divine nature.)

When this sacrament is afterwards really received, grace is increased and perfected but in a different way from Confirmation which increases and perfects grace to resist exterior attacks of Christ's enemies: whilst in this sacrament grace is so increased and spiritual life perfected that man may become perfect in himself in his interior life by union with God.

Obj. II. As bodily refreshment is taken to enable a man to use the physical strength he has, rather than to give him this strength, so it would appear that this sacrament of spiritual refreshment is given to us to enable us to use the grace we have already, rather than to impart new grace to us.

Reply. When the Eucharist bestows (an increase of) the virtue of charity, it also confers grace. Hence St John Damascene compares this sacrament to a burning coal which Isaias saw (6, 6). 'For a live ember is not simply wood, but wood united to fire; so also the bread of communion is not simply bread, but bread united with the divinity.'

And St Gregory says: 'God's love is never idle; and wherever present, it does great works.' Accordingly this sacrament not only confers sanctifying grace and the good habits called virtues; it also stirs up men to action according to the words of St Paul: '*The charity of Christ urges us*' (2 Cor. 5, 14); and therefore by this sacrament, the soul is spiritually refreshed and delighted, and, as it were, inebriated by the sweetness of the divine goodness according to the words of the Canticle, '*Eat, O my friends and be inebriated my dearly beloved.*'[1]

Obj. III. Our body is not a subject of grace; but as it

1 See pp. 95, 113.

was said above, Christ's body is offered for the salvation of our body, and the blood for the life of our soul (74. 1).

Reply. Sacraments operate just as they signify; therefore by a kind of assimilation, the body is said to be offered for the salvation of our body and the blood for our soul. But although each works for the salvation of both, since under both Christ is whole and entire (cf. 76, 2); and granted the body is not the immediate subject of grace, still its effect flows from the soul into the body whilst we present *our members as instruments of justice unto God* (Rom. 6, 13) in this life; and in the next, our body will share in the incorruption and glory of the soul.

Is the attaining of Glory an effect of this Sacrament? (Q. 79, 2)

Yes. St John says, '*If any man eat of this bread, he shall live for ever.*' But to live for ever is the life of glory: therefore the effect of this sacrament is the attainment of glory.

This effect is obtained, first, because Christ is present in this sacrament; secondly, the Passion is represented by it, thirdly, through the use of the sacrament and its species. [1]

Christ by his Passion opened the approach to life everlasting according to the Hebrews 9, 15. '*He is the Mediator. . . . That by means of his death, they that are called may receive the promise of eternal inheritance.*'

Again the refreshment of spiritual food and the unity signified by the species are to be had imperfectly here, but perfectly in glory.

Hence St Augustine's comment on the words '*My flesh is meat indeed*' (John 6, 56). 'Men seek in food and drink not to hunger or to thirst; but it is truly vain except (in) this food and drink which make those who partake of it immortal and incorruptible.'

---

[1] By frequent reception of the Blessed Sacrament, visits, exposition, processions, congresses.

Obj. I. An effect is proportioned to its cause; but this sacrament belongs to wayfarers, and hence is called Viaticum. But wayfarers are not yet capable of glory: therefore this sacrament does not cause its attainment,

Reply. Christ's Passion in virtue of which this sacrament is accomplished, is indeed a sufficient cause of glory. Yet not so that we are admitted by it at once to glory; but we must suffer *with him* in order that we may also be *glorified afterwards with him.* (Rom. 8, 17).

So also this sacrament does not immediately admit us to glory; but gives us the power to attain to it. Therefore it is called Viaticum; and a figure of it was Elias, who, because he ate and drank (a certain food), and in the strength of that same food, *walked forty days and forty nights unto the mount of God Horeb* (3 Kings 19, 8).

Obj. II. Many receive this sacrament who will never come to glory, according to St Augustine (*De Civ. Dei*, XXI). Therefore this sacrament is not the cause of attaining to glory.

Reply. As Christ's Passion does not produce its effect in those whose attitude towards it is not as it ought to be: so also they do not attain to glory through this sacrament who receive it unworthily.

Hence St Augustine explaining the same text says: '*The sacrament is one thing; its actual efficacy another. Many receive it from the altar; and by receiving, die. Eat then spiritually the heavenly bread. Bring innocence to the altar.*' It is not surprising then if those who do not preserve their innocence do not obtain the effect of this sacrament.

Obj. III. The greater is not brought about by the lesser. But it is lesser to receive Christ under a different species than to enjoy him in his own which belong to glory. Therefore this sacrament does not cause attainment to glory.

Reply. The fact that Christ is received under another species, is due to the nature of a sacrament which acts instrumentally. But from what was said above there is nothing to prevent an instrumental cause when employed by a higher agent from producing an effect beyond its own innate capacity (cf. III Q. 67, 3 ad 3).

Is forgiveness of mortal sin an effect of this Sacrament?
(Q. 79, 3)

Not in one who is conscious of mortal sin, for '*He that eateth and drinketh unworthily eateth and drinketh judgment to himself*' (1 Cor. 11, 29). According to the gloss, 'He eats and drinks unworthily who is in grievous sin; or who handles this sacrament irreverently.' Therefore, he who is in mortal sin heaps sin on sin by receiving the sacrament, instead of obtaining forgiveness.

The power of this sacrament can be considered in two ways: first, in itself; secondly, in the recipient. First, in itself, it has the power of forgiving sins from the Passion which is the fount and cause of forgiveness. Secondly, in the recipient, either there is, or there is not, an obstacle to receiving the fruit of this sacrament.

If conscious of mortal sin, he has within him an obstacle to receiving the effect of this sacrament. For he is not alive *spiritually*, and nourishment is confined to the living. And again he cannot be *united* with Christ, the effect of the sacrament, as long as he is attached to mortal sin. Hence it is said, 'If the mind has any affection for sinning *actually*,[1] it is burdened rather than purified by partaking of the Eucharist.' (*Eccles. Dogma*, C. 53.)

Therefore, this sacrament does not cause forgiveness in him who is conscious of mortal sin. But still this sacrament can affect forgiveness in two ways. First, by being received, not actually, but in desire, as when anyone is

1 MS. A. L. '*in actu*'. Other mss. commonly omit this word.

first justified from sin. Secondly, when received by a man
in mortal sin of which he is not conscious, and for which
he has no affection. Since probably he was not sufficiently
contrite at first, but by approaching with reverence and
devotion he obtains the grace of charity, which will perfect his contrition and remit sin.

Obj. I. In one of the collects it is said 'May this sacrament be a cleansing from crimes.' But mortal sins are
called crimes; therefore they are washed away by this
sacrament.

Reply. By crimes here are meant those of which we are
not conscious according to Psalm 18, 13: *'From my
hidden sins cleanse me, O Lord.'* Hence by this sacrament our
contrition may be perfected or strength may be given to
avoid sin.

Obj. II. This sacrament works by the power of Christ's
Passion just as Baptism does. But Baptism remits mortal
sins; so also should this sacrament, especially since it is
said in its form *'which shall be shed for many for the remission
of sins'.*

Reply. Baptism is spiritual re-birth, and a change from
spiritual non-being to spiritual being; and is given by way
of *ablution.* Therefore he who is conscious of mortal sin
does not improperly approach Baptism. But by this
sacrament a man takes Christ within himself by way of
spiritual nourishment, which is not adapted to one who is
dead in sin. There is therefore no parity.

Obj. III. Grace is given by this sacrament as said above
(Article 1). But a man is justified by grace from mortal
sin according to Romans 3, 24, *'Being justified freely by
his grace.'* Therefore mortal sins are remitted by this
sacrament.

Reply. (Sanctifying) grace is a sufficient cause of forgiveness of mortal sin but does not actually remit it unless

the sinner first receives this grace; which is not given in the Eucharist in this way.

Are Venial Sins forgiven through this Sacrament? (Q. 79, 4)

Yes, Innocent III says, '*The Eucharist blots out venial sins and guards against mortal.*'

Two things are to be considered: the sacrament itself and its peculiar effect. From both it appears that this sacrament can remit venial sins; for it is received under the appearances of nourishing food.

But bodily nourishment is needed to restore to the body what is lost every day by the action of natural heat: spiritually, also, something is wasted in us by the heat of concupiscence, by venial sins which diminish the fervour of charity, as was seen in the second part (II, II, 24, 10). So it belongs to this sacrament to remit venial sins.

Hence St Ambrose says, 'This daily bread is taken as a remedy for daily infirmity.'

The eminent effect of this sacrament is charity not only in habit but also in act which is aroused in this sacrament; and in this way venial sins are forgiven.

Obj. I. Contrary is taken away by contrary; but venial sins are not contrary to charity as shown in the second part (1, 2, 88, 1 ad 2; 2, 2, 24, 10). Since the Eucharist is the sacrament of charity, venial sins are therefore not forgiven by this sacrament.

Reply. Venial sins are not opposed to the *habit* of charity; they are opposed to the fervour of its act; and as the fervour of its act is enkindled by this sacrament, accordingly, venial sins are removed.

Obj. II. If any venial sins are forgiven by this sacrament, all of them are: But St John says, '*If we say that we have no sins we deceive ourselves*' (1-1-8).

Reply: This text does not mean that a man could not at some hour be without any guilt of venial sin; but it means that the just do not live all their lives free from venial sin.

Obj. III. Contraries (when of equal potency) mutually expel each other. But St Augustine says, '*Bring innocence to the altar: your sins though they be daily, let them not be deadly.*' Therefore neither are venial sins blotted out in this sacrament.

Reply. This is the sacrament of charity. Now the potency of charity is greater than venial sin. Therefore venial sin cannot totally impede that act. The same reasoning holds for this sacrament (as for charity).

Does this Sacrament remit the entire punishment due to sin?

(Q. 79, 5)

No. If it did, no other punishment should be inflicted, as none is inflicted on the newly baptized.

Now the Eucharist is a sacrament and a sacrifice. As a *sacrifice* it is *offered*, as a *sacrament it is received*.

The effect of the sacrament is felt in the recipient; and the effect of the sacrifice in the offerer, or in those for whom it is offered.

First, let us take it as a sacrament. As such, it produces primarily and directly that effect for which it was instituted. Now as nourishment is united with the person nourished, this sacrament was primarily and directly instituted to nourish men spiritually by union with Christ. But because this union with Christ is brought about by means of charity, and because in proportion to the fervour of his charity a man has remitted to him not alone his venial guilt, but also a certain measure of the punishment due; hence, as a result, and by way of a natural concomitant of the primary effect, Holy Communion also remits temporal punishment, not always in its entirety, but according to the measure of the fervour of the devotion of each communicant.

But as a sacrifice, the Blessed Eucharist, that is, the Holy Sacrifice of the Mass, has the power of cancelling our debts of temporal punishment; but here we should note that it is the affection or fervour of the offerer which is taken into account rather than the greatness of the thing offered. Therefore our Lord said of the widow, who offered the two mites, '*She cast in more than all the others*' (Luke 21, 4). Hence, though under the aspect of its own inherent greatness this sacrifice would suffice for the remission of all punishment, it actually works this remission only according to the measure of the devotion of those who offer it and of those for whom it is offered.

Obj. I. Man is forgiven all temporal punishment in Baptism by virtue of the effect of Christ's Passion. So also should he receive the same forgiveness in the Eucharist through which the effects of the Passion are also applied to him.

Reply. Baptism is instituted and directly intended to remit both guilt and temporal punishment. The Blessed Eucharist is instituted and directly intended for something quite different; for Baptism is given to a man as he is, as it were, dying to sin together with Christ. But Holy Communion is given to nourish and perfect him spiritually through Christ. Hence there is no parity.

Obj. II. Pope Alexander I says, '*No sacrifice can be greater than the body and blood of Christ.*' But in the Old Law it is written '*If a man shall sin let him offer* (this or that) *for his sin and it shall be forgiven him*' (Lev. 4, 5). Therefore this sacrament should avail much more for the remission of all punishment.

Reply. The sacrifices of the old law *did not remit* the whole punishment; for in greatness of victim they fell far[1] short of this our sacrifice, and on the side of personal

---

[1] This reply is a paraphrase of the words of St Thomas: 'The quantity of the thing offered did not remit the whole punishment as this sacrament does.'

G

devotion of the offerers, which restricts the effects even of our divine sacrifice, offerers under the old dispensation had their limitations too.

Obj. III. It is certain that some part of the debt of punishment is remitted by this sacrament; for sometimes by way of satisfaction a man is commanded to have Masses offered up for himself. But if one part of the punishment is forgiven, so is the other; for Christ's infinite power is contained in this sacrament. It seems therefore that the Eucharist can take away the whole punishment.

Reply. If part and not the whole of the temporal punishment is taken away, it is not because of any defect of Christ's power but in man's devotion.

Is Man preserved by this Sacrament from future sins?
(Q. 79, 6)

Yes. Our Lord said: '*This is the bread which cometh down from Heaven; that if any man eat of it he may not die*' (John 6, 50).

Evidently he does not mean the death of the body, but that this bread preserves from spiritual death through sin. For sin is the spiritual death of the soul; and man is preserved from future sin in the same way as the body is preserved from future death in two ways: first, from interior decay, by food and medicine; and secondly by weapons from exterior attacks.

Now this sacrament preserves us from sin in both these ways. For when man unites himself to Christ, through grace, the Eucharist is a spiritual food and medicine that strengthens his spiritual life according to the words '(This) bread strengthens man's heart' (Ps. 10, 35), and St Augustine says, '*Approach without fear, it is bread not poison*'. Secondly, it repels all the attacks of demons; since it is a sign of Christ's Passion by which devils are vanquished. Hence St Chrysostom says, '*We go from that table like lions breathing fire, being made terrible to the devil'* (*Hom. xlvi in Joann.*).

Obj. I. Many receive this sacrament worthily and afterwards fall into sin; this would not happen if this sacrament preserves from future sin.

Reply. The effect follows man's condition; just as the effect of every other active cause does, which is received in matter. But such is the condition of man on earth that his free will can be bent to good and evil. Hence although this sacrament can preserve from sin, it does not take away the possibility of sinning.

Obj. II. The Eucharist is the sacrament of charity. But charity can be lost through sin. Therefore this sacrament does not appear to preserve one from sin.

Reply. St Paul says, '*The love of your neighbour worketh no evil*' (Rom. 13, 10). So charity of itself keeps man from sinning; but a man sins after possessing charity, just as after receiving the Eucharist, owing to the mutability of free will.

Obj, III. The lessening of concupiscence is not given as an effect of this sacrament but rather of Baptism. Therefore preservation from sin is not an effect of this sacrament.

Reply. Although the Eucharist is not directly ordained to lessen concupiscence yet it does by the fact that it increases charity; '*For the increase of charity*', says St Augustine, '*is the diminution of concupiscence*'. But it directly strengthens man's heart in good; and he is therefore preserved from sin.

Does this Sacrament benefit others as well as the recipients?
(Q. 79, 7)

Yes. In the celebration of this sacrament prayer is offered for many others, which would be in vain unless this sacrament can also benefit those who do not receive it.

As said above (3) the Eucharist is not only a sacrament but also a sacrifice. As a sacrifice, Christ's Passion is represented whereby he offered himself a victim to God (Ephes. 5, 2). As a sacrament, invisible grace is bestowed under visible species.

First. Those who receive it are benefited by it in two ways: by the sacrament and by the sacrifice; because it is offered for all who partake of it. For, it is said in the Canon of the Mass: 'May as many of us as by participation at this altar shall receive the most sacred body and blood of thy Son, be filled with all heavenly benediction and grace.'

Second. As to others who do not receive, they are also benefited by way of sacrifice since it is offered for their salvation. Hence again it is said in the Canon of the Mass: 'Be mindful, O Lord, of thy servants, men and women ... for whom we offer, or who offer up to thee this sacrifice of praise for themselves and for all their own, for the redemption of their souls, for the hope of their safety and salvation.'

Third. Our Lord showed how we benefited in both ways by saying *which for you*, i.e., who receive it, *and for many*, i.e. others, *shall be shed unto the remission of sins.*

Obj. I. The Eucharist is of the same order as the other sacraments. But they can benefit only the recipients; for instance, only the person baptized receives the effect of Baptism. Therefore the Eucharist benefits only the recipient.

Reply. This sacrament is what the others are not. It is also a sacrifice. Therefore there is no parity.

Obj. II. If the Eucharist produces its effects in others as well as the recipient, a man might acquire grace, glory, and remission of sin through another receiving or offering this sacrament, and doing nothing himself.

Reply. Christ's Passion benefits all for the remission of sin, grace, and glory. But to produce its effects, we must be united with the Passion by faith and charity; and the same holds for this sacrifice, which is the memorial of the Passion. Therefore St Augustine says, *'Who may offer Christ's body except for them who are Christ's members?'* Hence no prayer is made in the Canon of the Mass for those outside of the Church.[1] But it benefits those who are (members) more or less according to the measure of their devotion.

Obj. III. Multiply the cause and you multiply the effect. If this sacrament benefits others, it follows that it would benefit a man more by receiving many Hosts consecrated in one Mass.

Reply. The effect is not increased since there is only *one* sacrifice; and only *one* Christ is present under *all* the Hosts and under *one*. But the oblation of the sacrifice is multiplied in many Masses; therefore the effect of the sacrifice and sacraments is multiplied.

Is the effect of this Sacrament impeded by Venial Sin? (Q. 79, 8)

Yes. St John Damascene says, *'The fire of that desire in us which is taken from the burning coal (i.e. from the Eucharist) will burn away our sins and set our hearts aglow, so that we ourselves shall be all on fire and become deified.'*

But the fire of our desire is damped by venial sins which cool the fervour of charity (cf. 1, 2, 8; 2, 2, 24, 10). That is, if they are actually being committed. For if past, they do not impede the effect of the sacrament[2] as it is possible for a man to approach it devoutly, and fully secure its effects in spite of even many past venial sins. But if

---

1 Still at the offering of the chalice the priest says: '*May it ascend for our salvation and that of the whole world in the odour of sweetness.*'

2 When younger, St Thomas taught the contrary, viz., that past venial sins did impede the effect of the Eucharist (cf. In sentent, IV, Dist. 12, Q. 2, Art. 10).

actually being committed, venial sins do in part, but not completely, hamper the effect of the sacrament. For, as said above (79, 1), the sacramental effect is not only to obtain grace or charity, but also to obtain a certain actual refreshment of spiritual sweetness, which is lessened if anyone approach this sacrament with mind distracted by venial sin, but the increase of habitual grace or of charity is not taken away.

Obj. I. St Augustine says, '*Eat the heavenly bread spiritually. Bring innocence to the altar. Your sins though they be daily let them not be deadly.*' But they who eat spiritually receive the effect of the sacrament. Therefore venial sins do not hinder its effect.

Reply. He who approaches with actual venial sin eats spiritually in *habit*, but not in *act*. He receives, therefore, the *habitual*, but not the *actual* effect of this sacrament.

Obj. II. This sacrament is not less powerful than Baptism. But only deception impedes the effect of Baptism; and venial sins do not belong to pretence, because '*The Holy Spirit will flee from the deceitful*' (Wis. 1, 5). Yet he is not put to flight by venial sins. Therefore they do not impede the effect of this sacrament.

Reply. Baptism is not ordained as this sacrament is to produce the fervour of charity. By Baptism the first perfection is acquired which is a habit. But this sacrament is spiritual eating which has actual delight.

Obj. III. Nothing removed by the action of any cause can impede its effect. But venial sins are taken away by this sacrament. Therefore they do not hamper its effect.

Reply. This reasoning refers to past venial sins which are taken away by this sacrament.

CHAPTER VIII

THE USE OF THIS SACRAMENT

Are there two distinct ways of eating Christ's Body? (Q. 80, 1)
YES.[1] In the reception of this sacrament, two things are to
be considered: the sacrament and its effect. Consequently
there are two ways of eating, sacramental and spiritual.

The reception is perfect if one obtain the effects, and
imperfect if prevented from receiving them; and just as
perfect is opposed to imperfect, so sacramental eating
alone is opposed to spiritual eating by which one receives
the effect of this sacrament and is thereby united with
Christ through faith and charity.

Obj. I. There are no two distinct ways of receiving
Baptism, viz., sacramentally and spiritually: neither
should there be in the Eucharist.

Reply. The same distinction holds in Baptism and the
other sacraments, namely, the sacrament only, and the
sacrament and its crowning effect. But whilst this sacrament is perfected by the *consecration* of the matter—the
others are perfected by its *use*. Again Baptism and some
other sacraments imprint a character which the Eucharist
does not. Therefore in this sacrament, the sacramental use
is distinguished from the spiritual more than in Baptism.

Obj. II. Sacramental eating is ordained for spiritual eating as its end. Therefore sacramental eating ought not to
be distinguished from spiritual.

1 St Thomas cites a gloss on the words '*He that eateth and drinketh unworthily*'
(1 Cor. 11, 29), to prove this affirmative, viz., 'We hold that there are two
ways of eating, the one, *sacramental*, and the other *spiritual*.'

Reply. Sacramental eating which tends to the spiritual is not distinguished from, but rather included under it. But that sacramental eating which does not obtain its effect is distinguished from the spiritual just as the perfect is singled out from the imperfect which does not attain to the perfection of its species.

Obj. III. Sacramental eating would be unnecessary if spiritual eating could be had without it.

Reply. The actual reception of the sacrament produces more fully the fruit of the sacrament than the mere desire, as said above of Baptism (69, 4 ad 2).

Does it belong to man alone to eat this Sacrament spiritually?
(Q. 80, 2)

Yes. St Augustine says: '*Eat spiritually the bread of the altar. Bring innocence to it. The angels do not approach the altar to take anything from it.*' Therefore they do not eat spiritually.

Now as Christ is not contained in this sacrament under his own, but under the sacramental species, there are consequently two ways of eating spiritually.

First. The angels eat Christ himself spiritually under his proper species because they are united to him in the enjoyment of perfect charity and in clear vision, which is the bread we wish for in Heaven.

Second. But here we are united to Christ by faith, and therefore eat him spiritually under the sacramental species, by believing in him, while desiring to receive this sacrament. This is not merely to eat Christ spiritually but to eat also this sacrament spiritually which is not the privilege of the angels.

Obj. I. But the psalmist says, '*Man ate the bread of angels*' (77, 55). That is according to the gloss, '*The body of Christ, who is truly the food of angels.*'

Reply. We receive Christ that we may enjoy him in

Heaven as the angels do. This is the end in view: which often is named from that which tends to it.

Obj. II. It may be inferred from St Augustine that angels eat this sacrament spiritually as well as men when he says: '*Christ wishes us to understand that this food and drink . . . is the fellowship of his members*' to which the angels also belong.

Reply. Men belong to the fellowship of his mystical body by faith; the angels by clear vision. But all the sacraments are proportioned by faith by *which the truth is seen through a glass and in a dark manner*. So properly speaking, it is men and not angels who eat this sacrament spiritually.

This reply also meets the third objection from St Augustine: '*Christ is to be eaten spiritually*.' For Christ says: '*He that eateth my flesh . . . abideth in me and I in him.*' But does Christ not also dwell in the holy angels by charity, and they in him? Yes, by *manifest vision*, but in men through *faith*. So there is no similarity.

Is it only a just man who can eat Christ Sacramentally?
(Q. 80, 3)

Sinners eat the body of Christ sacramentally and not the just only. For St Augustine says: '*Many receive from the altar and, by receiving, die.*' That is, those who die are sinners.

Formerly, some imagined that the body of Christ was not even sacramentally received by sinners, but that the moment it touches the lips of the unjust, it ceases to be under the sacramental species.

This is erroneous, because it takes away from the truth of the sacrament that as long as the species remain, the body of Christ does not cease to be under them (cf. 76, 6 ad 3).

But the species remain as long as the substance would, if it were there, as said above (77, 5, 8).

Now it is evident that the substance of bread taken by a sinner does not immediately cease to be, but lasts until digested by natural heat. Hence Christ's body remains just as long under the sacramental species when taken by sinners.

Obj. I. St Augustine says, '*To believe in him is to eat the living bread.*' But the sinner does not believe in him because he has not a living or *formed* faith, to which it belongs to believe in God, as said in the second part (II, II, 2-4). Therefore the sinner cannot eat this sacrament which is the living bread.

Reply. These words refer to spiritual eating which does not belong to sinners; for by it one receives the effect of this sacrament; and is thereby united with Christ through faith and charity. Hence the error, through ignorance of the distinction between this spiritual eating and corporal eating.

Obj. III. The sinner is more abominable to God than any irrational creature, for it is said of the sinner: '*Man when he was in honour did not understand—he hath been compared to senseless beasts and made like them*' (P. 47, 21). But a mouse cannot receive this sacrament just as it cannot receive Baptism. Therefore it seems for a similar reason sinners may not eat this sacrament.

Reply. If a mouse were to eat a consecrated Host the substance of Christ's body would remain as long as the substance of the bread would have remained. Nor does this point to any indignity since he willed to be crucified by sinners without any loss of his dignity.

An irrational creature cannot be said to eat *sacramentally* since it is incapable of using the Eucharist as a sacrament. Hence it eats Christ's body *accidentally* and not *sacramentally*, just as if one did not know a Host was consecrated and consumed it. And since what happens only accident-

THE USE OF THIS SACRAMENT

ally is not taken into account in essential divisions and distinctions, this mode of eating Christ's body is not set down as a third way in addition to sacramental and spiritual eating.

Does one not in the state of Grace sin in receiving Christ's Body Sacramentally? (Q. 80, 4)

The gloss says Yes, on the passage (1 Cor. 11, 29), '*He that eateth and drinketh unworthily eateth and drinketh judgment to himself.*'

He eats and drinks unworthily who is in sin or who treats it irreverently.

There is a twofold reality of this sacrament as said above: one which is *signified and contained*, namely Christ himself, and another which is *signified* but *not contained*, that is, Christ's mystical body or fellowship of the saints.

Whoever receives this sacrament, thereby signifies that he is one with Christ and incorporated with his members by a *formed* or living faith, which no one has, who is in mortal sin. It is clear then that whoever receives the Eucharist in the state of mortal sin becomes a liar to this sacrament and is guilty of a sacrilege.

Obj. I. Christ has no greater dignity under the sacramental species than under his own. But sinners who touched Christ's body under its proper species did not sin, but on the contrary obtained forgiveness of sin. Therefore the sinner by receiving sacramentally does not sin but rather obtains salvation.

Reply. Christ on earth did not give himself to men to be touched as a sign of spiritual union as he does to those who receive him in this sacrament. Therefore sinners who touched him in his proper species were not guilty of lying to things divine as sinners do who receive this sacrament. Moreover Christ still bore the likeness of the flesh of sin, and therefore fittingly allowed himself to be touched by sinners. But once the flesh of sin was removed by the glory of the Resurrection, he forbade the woman to touch[1] him, because her faith in him was defective according to St John: 'Do not touch me for I am not ascended to my father', namely, 'in your heart', as St Augustine says. Therefore sinners who are deficient in *formed* faith or living faith in Christ are debarred from touching this sacrament.

Obj. II. This sacrament, like others is spiritual medicine. But medicine is given to the infirm according to St Matthew: '*They that are in health need not a physician*'; and those that are spiritually sick are sinners. Therefore they can receive this sacrament without sin.

Reply. Every medicine does not suit every stage of sickness. What is given in the convalescent stage would be hurtful whilst the fever is raging. So Baptism and Penance are as purgative medicine to take away the fever of sin. But this sacrament is a strengthening medicine to be given only to those who are free from grievous sin.

Obj. IV. If a sinner sins by receiving this sacrament, so also should one who beholds it. But this is clearly false since the Church exposes this sacrament to be seen and adored by all; therefore the sinner does not sin by receiving it.

Reply. The body of Christ is not received by being seen; for sight does not penetrate the substance of Christ's body, but only the sacramental species as said above (76, 7). But he who eats not only receives the sacramental species but he also receives Christ himself.

Obj. V. A sinner is sometimes not aware of his sins. But

---

1 That is according to the Latin Vulgate: 'Noli me tangere'—but not according to the Greek version 'μή μον 'ἅπτον' which means: 'Do not cling to me.' As much as to say 'Let my feet go now, later on you will be able to grasp my feet and kiss them often before I ascend to my Father.' (Cf. à Lapide, John 20, 17.)

if he sins by receiving the Eucharist, so also should every-one else, since they expose themselves to the danger; for the apostle says '*I am not conscious to myself of anything, yet I am not hereby justified*' (1 Cor. 4, 4).

Reply. One can be unaware of his sin by his own fault either by inexcusable ignorance; for instance if one thinks fornication is not a mortal sin, or by neglecting to exam-ine himself as the Apostle enjoins: '*Let a man prove himself and so let him eat of that bread and drink of the chalice*' (1 Cor. 11, 28). In either case the sinner by receiving the body of Christ is guilty of a crime although unconscious of his sin; because with him his very ignorance is sinful.

On the other hand it may happen without any fault of his own, when for instance he was not sufficiently contrite; in such a case, he does not sin by receiving the body of Christ because no man knows for certain if he is really contrite. It is sufficient if he finds in himself such signs of contrition as to be sorry for past sins and resolves to avoid them in future.

Is it the greatest of all crimes to approach this Sacrament con-scious of (mortal) Sin? (Q. 80, 5)

No. Unbelief appears to be the greatest. For St Augus-tine says the words: '*If I had not come and had not spoken to them they would be without sin*' are to be understood of the sin of unbelief *in which all sins are contained*, as stated in the second part (2, 2, 73).

One sin is graver than another either of its own nature or accidentally. First, of itself: The gravity of the sin depends on the object. The greater the object the greater the crime committed against it. Hence since Christ's divinity is greater than his humanity, and his humanity greater than the *sacraments* of his humanity; the greatest sins are those against his Godhead such as unbelief and blasphemy: in a lesser degree those against his humanity;

in the third place those against the sacraments belong to Christ's humanity and after these, the other sins against pure creatures.

Accidentally, one sin can be greater than another on the part of the sinner. For instance a sin even of wilful ignorance or weakness is lighter than one of contempt or committed with sure knowledge.

The same reason holds for other circumstances. Thus to receive the sacrament with actual contempt and consciousness of sin is a greater crime than to approach with some consciousness of guilt, but from fear of the sin being discovered.

Obj. I. St Paul says: '*Whoever shall eat of this bread unworthily shall be guilty of the body and blood of the Lord*' (I Cor. II, 27), and the gloss on this says, 'He shall be punished as though he murdered Christ'.

But the sin of the murderers of our Lord is *most grave*. Therefore the same holds for those who approach Christ's table conscious of sin.

Reply. The sin of Christ's executioners is much greater. First, because it was against his sacred body in its own species; whilst the sin of the unworthy recipient is against it under the sacramental species. Secondly, because the executioners by their sins meant to injure Christ, whilst the unworthy recipient does not. The meaning, therefore, of St Paul and of the gloss is that the sin of the unworthy recipient is compared to the actual killing of Christ by way of similitude.

Obj. II. The fornicator approaching Christ's table appears to sin as Judas did; that is, very gravely; and there are other sins still graver than fornication, especially the sin of unbelief; therefore the crime of any sinner approaching the altar is the gravest of all, since, like Judas, he betrays the Son of Man.

Reply. The fornicator receiving Christ is put on a par with Judas kissing Christ; because each outrages him with the sign of affection. But Judas's sin was the greater. The resemblance to crime applies to other sinners as well as to fornicators; for all act against the charity of Christ of which this sacrament is the sign. But in a way, the sin of fornication makes a man more unfit to receive this sacrament; because by this sin the spirit is utterly subjected to the flesh; and thus the fervour of love is impeded. But the impediment to charity weighs more than the impediment to fervour. Hence, the sin of unbelief fundamentally severs a man from the unity of the Church, and renders him completely unfit to receive *that* which is the sacrament of unity, as said above (67, 2). Hence the unbeliever errs more grievously and despises Christ all the more by receiving and not believing in his real presence than one who does believe, but receives him in sin. For the unbeliever as far as he can makes little of the holiness of the sacrament and of the power of Christ, whilst the guilty believer, who receives this sacrament despises it not in *itself,* but in its *use.*

Hence, the apostle shows how one is guilty of the body of the Lord by *not discerning* it; that is, by not distinguishing it from other food, and this is what the unbeliever does.

Ought the Priest to deny the Body of Christ to the sinner who seeks it? (Q. 80, 6)

A distinction must be made. St Augustine commenting on the words of the Psalm, '*All the fat ones of the earth have eaten and have adored*' (21, 30) says, 'Let not the dispenser prevent the fat ones of the earth (i.e. sinners) from eating at the Lord's table.' By sinners here are meant those whose sins are not publicly known. Hence, Holy Communion should not be denied them if they ask for it. For no baptized Catholic may be deprived of his right to be admitted to the Lord's table unless for some manifest reason. Therefore again St Augustine says: 'We may not prohibit anyone from going to Communion unless he has openly confessed, or has been exposed and convicted by some lay or ecclesiastical court.'

But still a priest may warn a *secret* sinner *privately*, or *public* sinner *openly*, not to approach the Lord's table until they have repented, and have been reconciled to the Church; and if so, Communion must not be refused even to public sinners, especially at the hour of death.

Obj. I. Our Lord's command is: '*Give not that which is holy to dogs*' (Matt. 7, 6). But to give this sacrament to sinners is throwing holy things to dogs. Therefore not even to avoid defaming them publicly should the Eucharist be given to sinners.

Reply. Dogs here mean *notorious sinners.* But hidden crimes, however, cannot be publicly punished; but are to be left to the divine judgment.

Obj. II. One must choose the lesser of two evils. It seems a lesser evil if a sinner be defamed or an unconsecrated host be given to him, than for him to sin mortally by receiving the body of Christ.

Reply. It is worse to sin mortally by unjustly defaming the hidden sinner than for the sinner to sin grievously (by receiving).

Because a man ought not to commit a mortal sin to save someone else from being guilty of another. For, St Augustine says: '*A most dangerous barter is for us to do evil to prevent greater.*'

But the secret sinner should prefer to be defamed rather than approach the Lord's table unworthily. Yet, on no account should an unconsecrated host be given; because it would thereby make the communicant and others commit idolatry by believing that the host is consecrated. For, as St Augustine says: '*Let no one eat Christ's flesh without first adoring it*' (Ps. 98, 5).

Obj. III. Sometimes the body of Christ is given to suspects, to test their innocence or guilt. For instance, the decretals say: 'In case of theft in a monastery, the brethren to prove their innocence shall all communicate . . . after Mass in these words: "May the body of Christ be to me for a proof this day." ' (This rule was meant exclusively for religious, who by their calling should fear God before man, and who therefore would much prefer to admit a slight theft than thus solemnly call on Christ to prove a lie, by receiving him in Holy Communion.)

Reply. These decretals were annulled by the Popes, because in this act there seemed to be a tempting of God which cannot be done without sin: moreover it would seem a still more grave sin if the sacrament instituted as a means of salvation should become the cause of death.

Do nocturnal emissions prevent one from receiving this Sacrament? (Q. 80, 7)

Mortal sin alone necessarily prevents anyone from receiving the Eucharist.

These movements may be due first to an external spiritual cause; secondly, to an internal spiritual cause; thirdly to an external corporeal cause.

Each of these three causes can be without sin, or with venial sin, or with mortal sin.

If without sin, or with venial sin, it does not necessarily prevent the receiving of the Eucharist. First, an external spiritual cause comes from the demon who can stir up the imagination, as said in the first part (Q. 111, 3). But such satanic illusions may be due to neglect in preparation (to receive) with devotion; and this can be either a mortal or a venial sin.

H

Sometimes these illusions may come from sheer malice of the devils who wish to keep men from receiving the Sacrament. For Cassian tells us (Conf. XXII) that when a certain brother suffered defilement always on the feast days on which he should go to Communion, his superiors finding that he did nothing to cause it, decided he was not to stop going to the altar and the illusion ceased.

Secondly, internal spiritual causes such as previous evil thoughts may not be sinful at all; as when one has to read and debate on such things; and if not accompanied by concupiscence and pleasure, these thoughts are not unclean but blameless; and yet, on the authority of St Augustine, pollution can follow from them.

Thirdly, external corporeal causes such as come from bodily weakness or from the abundance of nature can be without sin. For, just as blood can flow without sin, so also the seed of nature which is superfluous blood can flow without sin. But sometimes this cause is with sin when due to excess of food or drink; and this sin may be venial or mortal.

If the cause is only venial, or not sinful, a sense of becomingness[1] should prevent one from receiving for two reasons: (a) bodily defilement, (b) mental distractions that follow nocturnal emissions—especially when it occurs with unclean phantasms. But in case of necessity neither of these reasons holds.

Obj. III. Venial sin or mortal sin after repentance is no obstacle to receiving Communion. But, suppose nocturnal pollution is due to some previous sin, for instance, gluttony or to an evil thought; generally such (seminal loss) is a venial sin; and occasionally if it be mortal, one may repent and confess it in the morning; therefore such a

---

[1] Medical authorities agree with St Thomas that these emissions are often the result of a pathological nervous condition.

one should not be prohibited from receiving this sacrament.

Reply. Although the stain of guilt is taken away by contrition and confession still the bodily defilement is not taken away nor the distraction of mind that follows it.

(Such was the received opinion in St Thomas's day; now the official teaching of the Church as given in the decree of 20th December, 1905, is:

Rule 1. Frequent and daily Communion as a thing most earnestly desired by Christ our Lord, and by the Catholic Church, should be open to all the faithful of whatever rank and condition of life, and that no one who is in the state of grace and who approaches the holy table with a right and devout intention can lawfully be hindered therefrom.

Rule 5. That the practice of frequent and daily Communion may be carried out with the greatest prudence, and more abundant merit, the confessor's advice should be asked. Confessors, however, are to be careful not to dissuade anyone from frequent and daily Communion *provided that he is in a state of grace and approaches with a right intention.*)

Does food or drink taken before this Sacrament prevent its reception? (Q. 80, 8)

There are two impediments to receiving this sacrament: mortal sin, which is opposed to what it signifies (cf. art. 4), and the prohibition of the Church against its reception after taking food or drink; and that, for three reasons:

First, because as St Augustine says: 'It was pleasing to the Holy Ghost that in honour of this sacrament the body of the Lord should enter the mouth of the Christians before any other food.'

Secondly, on account of what this sacrament signifies:

namely that Christ himself, who is the great central effect of this sacrament, and his charity should first be rooted in our hearts according to the words of St Matthew: '*Seek first the Kingdom of God.*'

Thirdly, on account of the danger of vomiting, or of drunkenness that may sometimes occur through eating or drinking to excess. Just as the apostle says: '*One is hungry, another is drunk*' (1 Cor. 11, 23). The sick are exempt from this general rule, if there be any danger of dying without Communion; because necessity has no law.

Obj. I. Our Lord gave this sacrament to his disciples after he dined (cf. Luke 21, 1 Cor. 11). Should we not also receive this sacrament after eating other food?

Reply. St Augustine says: 'It is not because the Lord gave this sacrament after other food that we should also receive it after dinner and supper as did those brethren whom the apostle reproves. For, in order to commend with all earnestness the depth of this mystery our Saviour wished to engrave this last (act) on the hearts and memories of his disciples; and therefore gave no command for it to be received in this order. That was for the apostles to arrange through whom he was to rule the Churches (Epist. ad Januar.).

Obj. IV. To take water or medicine or any other food in very slight quantities or the remains of food does not break the fast.

Reply. No matter how small the quantity, it is never lawful to receive this sacrament after taking food or drink or even medicine. But what remains left in the mouth of the food or of the water or wine used for washing the mouth, if not deliberately swallowed in great quantity, but mixed with the saliva, does not prevent one from receiving it.

Obj. VI.[1] No less reverence is due to the Eucharist after receiving it than before. But a man may eat and drink after receiving the sacrament. Therefore one may do so before receiving it.

Reply. The greatest devotion is required at the actual receiving of this sacrament; because then the effect of the sacrament is bestowed and such devotion is more impeded by what goes before than by what comes after. Hence men were to fast before receiving rather than after. But still there should be some interval between taking this sacrament and other food. Hence the post-Communion prayer of thanksgiving is said, and the communicants say their own private prayers.

An ancient Canon of Clement I was: 'If the Lord's portion was eaten in the morning, the ministers who receive it shall fast to the sixth hour.' For, in older times, Mass was said rarely and with greater preparation. But now owing to its being said oftener this (law) has been abrogated by a contrary custom, because it could not be easily observed.

Ought those to receive this Sacrament who have not the use of reason? (A. 80, 9).

The first Council of Orange decreed: 'All things that

---

[1] *Obj. V* refers to those who eat and drink late, or just before retiring to rest, and who possibly after a sleepless night receive Holy Communion in the morning when the food is not fully digested.

St Thomas replies: 'As far as precept is concerned it makes no matter whether the food is digested or not, but what does matter is that if the mind be much disturbed one may become unfit for receiving this sacrament.' This teaching is now to be interpreted by the second rule of the decree of 20th December, 1905, explaining the first rule that '*no one* is to be hindered from receiving who is in the state of grace and who approaches with a right intention'.

Rule 2. 'A right intention consists in this, that he who approaches the holy table should do so, not out of routine, or vainglory or human respect, but for the purpose of pleasing God, of being more closely united with him in charity.' Hence, as virtue is perfected in infirmity, one may even approach with a mind much disturbed, if he goes with the desire of pleasing God; and a proof would be if he felt more disturbed if he did not go.

belong to piety are to be given to the insane.' But this sacrament is the sacrament of piety, therefore it must be given to these.

Some lack the use of reason in two ways:

First: The feeble-minded who are like men who see dimly and therefore are said *not* to see. The Blessed Sacrament is *not* to be denied to these since they can conceive some devotion towards it.

Second: Those who never had the use of reason from birth. The sacrament is not to be given to these because in no way was there any preceding devotion.

There is yet another class who were not always devoid of reason: and if in their lucid movements they gave proof of devotion towards this sacrament, it ought to be given to them at the hour of death unless there is danger of vomiting.

St Thomas gives two objections: (1) Those possessed by the devil (*energumens*) were not even allowed to see the Eucharist. (2) Children just baptized did not receive it: therefore neither should anyone else who has not the use of reason.

Reply. Only those who were possessed, but not baptized, were prevented from looking at the Blessed Sacrament—as the devil's power was very active in them through the presence of original sin (they became violent in their efforts to get away from it). As regards infants, Dionysius said Holy Communion was to be given to the baptized—meaning adults; but some of the Greeks misinterpreting him give it also to children after Baptism. But they suffer no loss of life (by not actually receiving); for St Augustine says: 'Every believer is a partaker spiritually of the body and blood of the Lord when he becomes a member of Christ's body in Baptism.'

When children begin to have a *glimmer of reason so that*

they can conceive some devotion[1] then this sacrament can be given to them.

Is it lawful to receive this Sacrament daily? (Q. 80, 10)

Yes. '*This is our daily bread. Take it daily that it may profit thee daily*', says St Augustine.

The use of this sacrament may be either in regard to the sacrament itself or to the recipient.

First, as regards the sacrament: its virtue is helpful to men and therefore it is profitable to receive daily so as to partake of it daily.

Hence St Ambrose says: '*Christ's blood is shed for the forgiveness of sins: I who sin always ought to receive it always.*[2] *I need an ever-present remedy*' (*De Sacram.*, V). Secondly. As regards the recipient: he should approach with great devotion and reverence. If anyone finds himself disposed in this way to receive daily, it would be commendable to do so. For when Augustine says: '*Receive daily that it may profit thee daily*', he adds: '*So live as to deserve to receive it daily.*'

But there are often so many impediments arising from either a disordered mind or body, a great many have not this devotion, and therefore it is not expedient for all to go daily to the altar, but as often as they find themselves prepared. Hence it is said: 'I neither praise nor blame those who receive daily' (*De Eccles. Dogmat.* 53).

Since these words were written, the Council of Trent calls the Eucharist '*THE ANTIDOTE whereby we are delivered from daily faults and preserved from deadly sins*' (Sess. XIII, C. 2); and St Ambrose maintains that to hold

---

1 These words of St Thomas—Quando pueri incipiunt aliqualem usum rationis habere—were cited by Pius X in his famous decree of August 7th, 1910, viz., 'The age of discretion is reached when a child knows the difference between the bread which is the Holy Eucharist and ordinary material bread. . . . For incipient reason, that is to say *some use of reason*, suffices.'

2 By a spiritual communion when a sacramental is impossible.

back from Communion is not piety according to the spirit and teaching of Jesus Christ who has not said 'reverence it and keep away', but 'reverence it and draw nigh' (cf. Notes on frequent Communion, Zulueta, p. 29). According to the Decree of Pius X, one may approach, in spite of a disordered mind or body, if in the state of grace and with the right intention.

Obj. I. A person is baptized once only; for Christ died only once for our sins (1 Pet. 3, 18). Therefore it does not seem lawful to receive him daily.

Reply. Baptism imprints the character or seal of Christ, because by it man is conformed to Christ's death. But as Christ died once only, so man is baptized once only. In the Eucharist man does not receive Christ's character, but himself, whose strength endures for ever; and that strength man needs daily. Therefore he can commendably receive this sacrament every day. For, just as bodily food is taken daily, so it is a proper thing to receive this sacrament every day. Hence our Lord tells us to say, 'Give us this day our daily bread'; and St Augustine's comment on this is: 'If you receive daily (this sacrament), *daily*, is today for thee. Christ rises every day in thee; for *when Christ rises it is today.*' [1]

Obj. II. The truth and the figure should correspond; but the paschal lamb was the chief figure of this sacrament, as said above (73, 6), and was only eaten once a year. The Church only commemorates the Passion once a year; seemingly then this sacrament should be received only once a year.

Reply. Christ died but once, and the paschal lamb pre-

[1] That is, just as the sun rises every day, and because it rises, *it is today*. So, when we receive the Sun of Justice, it is *today* for us.

In the old churches, wherever the ruins remain, we may remark that the priest at the altar was always facing due east, i.e., the rising sun, typifying the Sun of Justice that rose daily there, in the morning sacrifice.

figured his death, and therefore was taken once a year only. For the same reason the Church commemorates the Passion once a year only. But in the Eucharist the memorial of the Passion is given by way of food, which is daily consumed, and therefore is typified by the manna which was given to the people in the desert.

Obj. III. The greatest reverence is due to this sacrament, which contains the whole Christ. But reverence demands that one should abstain from receiving it. For the centurion was praised for saying: 'Lord, I am not worthy that thou shouldst enter under my roof' (Matt. 8, 8), and Peter for exclaiming: 'Depart from me for I am a sinful man, O Lord' (Luke 5, 8). Therefore he who receives daily is not to be commended.

Reply. The reverence due to this sacrament is fear joined to love, and is called filial fear; because it regards God, as said in the second part (2, 2, 19). Now the desire of partaking springs from love, and the humility of reverence comes from fear. Therefore both belong to reverence, whether in receiving this sacrament daily, or sometimes by abstaining from it. Hence St Augustine says: 'If one man holds that the Eucharist is not to be received daily, and another the contrary, let each act according to what his faith piously believes should be done.' For Zaccheus and the centurion did not contradict each other, when the one received the Lord with joy and the other said: '*I am not worthy that thou shouldst enter under my roof*'. But love and hope are preferable to fear: hence when Peter said: 'Depart from me for I am a sinful man', our Lord answered: 'Fear not'.

Obj. V. The Church requires Communion only once a year; therefore it is not commendable to receive daily.

Reply. The laws varied according to the different state of the Church. In the beginning when devotion was more vigorous the rule was to receive daily. Hence Pope Anacletus says: 'After consecration, let all communicate who do not wish to be outside the threshold of the Church; for so the apostles ordained, and the Holy Roman Church maintains.'

As the fervour of the faithful cooled, Pope Fabian allowed them to communicate if not more frequently at least at Easter, Pentecost, and Christmas; and Pope Soter commanded that Communion be received on Holy Thursday. Later on when iniquity abounded and charity grew cold, Pope Innocent III ordered that the faithful should receive at least once a year at Easter. However, the faithful are advised to communicate on all Sundays. (But now not only on Sundays but even daily when they can.)

Is it lawful to abstain altogether from Communion? (Q. 80, 11)

No. Our Lord said, '*Except you eat the flesh of the Son of Man and drink his blood you shall not have life in you*' (John 6, 54).

There are two ways of receiving: *spiritual* and *sacramental* (cf. 80, 1). All are bound to eat at least spiritually; because this is to be incorporated in Christ as said above (73, 3 ad 1). Now spiritual eating includes the desire to receive this sacrament (cf. ibid). *And if anyone has no desire to receive it he cannot be saved.* But a desire would be vain unless realized when the opportunity arises. Therefore a man is bound to receive this sacrament not only by the law of the Church but also by the command of the Lord: '*Do this in memory of me*' (Luke 22, 19); and the Church determines the time when that command is to be fulfilled.

Obj. I. The centurion is praised for saying: '*Lord, I am not worthy that thou shouldst enter under my roof.*' He who thinks that he ought to abstain altogether from Communion may be compared to this centurion (cf. 80, 10 ad 3). But no one ever read of Christ entering his house;

therefore it seems lawful for one to abstain during life from Communion.

Reply. St Gregory says: '*When a benefit is commanded to be accepted, true humility does not obstinately refuse.*' Hence it is not laudable humility to abstain from Communion against the command of the Church; and moreover the centurion was not told to receive Christ into his house.

Obj. II. This sacrament is not necessary for salvation as said above (Q. 73, 3). Therefore it is lawful to abstain from it.

Reply. Children can be saved without the (actual reception of the) Eucharist; yet not without Baptism. Both are of necessity to adults.

Is it lawful to receive the body of Christ under the species of bread without also receiving his blood under the species of wine? (Q. 80, 12)

Yes. It is the custom of many churches to give the body of Christ but not his blood.

This *use* of the sacrament regards the recipients and also the sacrament itself.

First, as to the sacrament itself: since its perfection consists in both the body and blood, on no account ought the priest to take the one without the other; for it is his duty to consecrate and consummate this sacrament.

Secondly, as to the recipient: extreme reverence and caution are needed lest anything should happen that would dishonour so great a mystery. For instance the blood if incautiously taken might be easily spilt. For there are multitudes of young and old (approaching the altar), and some of them may not be careful enough in using this sacrament. Hence in certain churches the priest alone receives the blood. (It is now the general custom in the Western Church to give Holy Communion under the species of the bread only. Some Catholics of the Eastern Rites communicate under both kinds.)

Obj. II.[1] Pope Gelasius says: 'The division of one and the same mystery cannot happen without a great sacrilege.' Therefore both the body and blood should be taken.

Reply. The perfection of this sacrament is not found in the *use* by the faithful but in the consecration of the matter: therefore the perfection is not lessened if the faithful take the body without the blood, provided the consecrating priest consumes both.

Obj. III. Christ's Passion is expressed in the blood rather than in the body; for the blood is offered for the health of the soul (cf. 74, 1). Therefore those who approach the altar ought not to take Christ's body without his blood.

Reply. The Passion is re-presented in the consecration itself wherein the body ought not to be consecrated without the blood. But the body can be received by the people without the blood; because the priest offers and consumes the blood on behalf of all; and Christ is whole and entire under both species as said above (76, 2).

---

1 *Obj. I* (omitted) refers to priests not taking the precious blood.

Chapter IX

HOW CHRIST USED THIS SACRAMENT
AT ITS INSTITUTION

Did Christ receive his own Body and Blood? (Q. 81, 1)
YES. St Jerome says: 'The Lord Jesus Christ himself,
the guest and banquet, is both the consumer and what is
consumed.

Some held that Christ gave his body and blood to his
disciples during the supper but did not take them himself. This seems to be unlikely. For Christ himself was the
first to observe what he wished others to do.

Therefore, he would have himself baptized first before
he imposed Baptism on others. Just as we read in the Acts:
'*Jesus began to do and to teach*' (1, 1). Hence again, he first
took his own body and blood and afterwards gave them
to his disciples; and the gloss commenting on the words
of Ruth 3, 7, '*When he had eaten and drunk*' says: 'Christ
ate and drank at the Supper, when he gave to his disciples
the sacrament of his body and blood.'

Obj. I. It is not said in the Gospels that Christ ate his
own body and drank his own blood. Therefore this is
not to be asserted (when there is no positive proof).

Reply. We read in the Gospels that Christ *took the bread
and the chalice.* But we are not to understand, as some say,
that he merely took them in his hands, but that he took
them in the same way as he gave them to others to take.
Therefore when he said: '*Take ye and eat. . . . Take ye and
drink*' it is to be understood that he also while taking it—
ate and drank; hence the couplet:

'Holding himself in his hands, with the twelve at
supper reclined,
He himself becomes his own food; with ardent desire
he dined.'[1]

Obj. II. What is eaten and drunk is in him who eats and
drinks. Therefore since the whole Christ is under each
species, it seems impossible for him to receive this
sacrament.

Reply. Christ is in this sacrament according to the
dimensions of the sacramental species, not according to
his own: so that wherever the species are, there also is the
whole Christ. Hence he could be in his hands and in his
mouth at the same time. This could not be if his relation
to space were according to his proper dimensions.

Obj. III. The reception of this sacrament is twofold:
spiritual and sacramental. The spiritual did not suit
Christ, as he derived nothing from the sacrament.
Neither did the sacramental, because it is imperfect without the spiritual (cf. 80, 1). Therefore Christ did not eat
this sacrament in any way.

Reply. As said above (79, 1 ad 2) the effect of this
sacrament is not only an increase of *habitual* grace, but
also a certain actual delight of spiritual sweetness.

But although Christ's grace could not be increased by
receiving this sacrament, yet he had a certain spiritual
delight from its new institution. Hence he says himself
(Luke 22, 15): '*With desire have I desired to eat this Pasch
with you.*' Therefore he ate it both spiritually and sacramentally, yet in a different way from the others who also
ate it sacramentally and spiritually. For they received an
increase of grace and they needed the sacramental signs
to perceive its truth.

1 Rex sedet in coena, turba cinctus duodena. Se tenet in manibus, se cibat
ipse cibus.

Did Christ give his own Body to Judas? (Q. 81, 2)

St Thomas says yes and quotes St John Chrysostom's words: 'Judas partook of the mysteries and was not converted.' But St Hilary held that Christ did not give his body to Judas and that it was only by right, considering the malice.[1]

St Thomas replies that as Christ was a pattern of justice it was not according to his teaching to repel Judas, a hidden sinner, without clear proof of guilt, lest prelates later on, might be encouraged to do likewise, and also, lest Judas being angered, might make his repulsion an excuse for turning traitor.

And if it be urged that our Lord said: '*Give not holy things to dogs*', St Thomas answers that as Judas's crime was known to Christ as God, and not as man knows it: he thus taught by example that secret sinners are not to be repelled by any priest.

Did Christ receive and give to his Disciples his impassible Body? (Q. 81, 3)

No. Innocent III says: 'He gave to his disciples the body such as he had it then.' Therefore it was a mortal and passible body he gave.

Hugh of St Victor[2] held that before his Passion, Christ assumed at different times the four properties of a glorified body, namely, subtlety, when he came from the closed womb of the Virgin; agility, when he walked

---

1 According to modern Commentators it seems more probable that Judas had gone out, so that John 13, 21, is identical with Matthew 26, 21; and both narratives are parallel to Matthew, verse 25, and John, verse 30. The one great proof in favour of St Thomas's opinion is St Luke 22, 20, when our Lord says immediately after the words of Consecration: '*But yet behold the hand of him that betrayeth me is with me on the table.*'

    Maldonatus holds that Judas was not a hidden sinner; for our Lord, by giving him bread dipped (John 13, 26), showed who was to be the traitor and exposed him when he exclaimed: '*Thou hast said it.*' (Matthew 26, 25).

2 A Canon Regular of Paris who died in 1140 at the age of 44 and was called a second Augustine.

with dry feet on the sea; splendour when transfigured; and impassibility at the last Supper, when he gave his body to the disciples to be eaten; and therefore he gave to his disciples a body that was impassible and immortal.

We have stated what should be held about the other qualities (III, Q. 28, 2 ad 3; and 45, 2), but what Hugh of St Victor says about impassibility is inadmissible.

For it is evident that the same true body of Christ then seen by the disciples in its own species was received by them under the sacramental species.

But in its own, it was not impassible, but rather was it prepared for the Passion: therefore Christ's body was not impassible under the sacramental species.

Still what was passible in itself was in the sacrament in an impassible manner, just as what was visible in itself was invisibly there.

For as sight demands that the body which is seen is in contact with the surrounding medium of vision: so does passibility require contact of the suffering body with what acts upon it. But Christ's body, as it is under the sacrament (cf. 1 ad 2, Q. 76), is not in relation with its surroundings, i.e., through the medium of its own dimensions, whereby bodies touch one another—but through the dimensions of the bread and wine. Therefore it is these species which are acted upon and seen, not Christ's own body.

Obj. I. Christ gave his body suitable for eating. Therefore he gave it just as it was after the Passion; that is, impassible and immortal. For the gloss on the words '*He was transfigured before them*' (Matt. 17, 2) says 'He gave at this Supper that body he had through nature but neither mortal nor passible'; and again on Lev. 2, 5, '*If the oblation be on the frying pan*' the gloss says '*The Cross*

... made Christ's flesh fit for eating which it did not seem to be before the Passion.'

Reply. Christ is said not to have given his mortal body and passible body at the Supper, because he did not give it in a mortal and passible way. But the Cross made Christ's flesh suitable for eating in as much as this sacrament represents his Passion.[1]

Obj. II. Every passible body suffers by contact and by being eaten: therefore if the body of Christ was passible, it would have suffered when eaten by the disciples.

Reply. This reasoning would hold if Christ's body were in a passible way in this sacrament just as it was then passible in itself.

Obj. III. Christ's impassible and immortal body is now on the altar by virtue of the sacramental words. It should have been much more so when these words were pronounced by Christ himself.

Reply. It is not by virtue of the sacrament that accidents such as impassibility are present, but by concomitance only. For, by virtue of the sacramental words the substance of the bread is changed into the body of Christ, whatever be the accidents which really exist in it.

Had this Sacrament been reserved, or consecrated at the time Christ died, would he also have died there? (Q. 81, 4)

Yes. The same Christ who was on the cross would have been in this sacrament. But he died on the cross. He would then have died in this sacrament if reserved in it.

The body of Christ is substantially[2] the same in this sacrament as in its own species, yet not in the same way. For in its own species it touches surrounding bodies by its own dimensions, but not so in this sacrament as said above (Art. 3).

---

1 In the Last Supper this sacrament *pre*-presented Christ's Passion.
2 'Substantially' here means *in its entire substance*.

J

Therefore all that belongs to Christ as he is in himself can be attributed to him both in his own species and as he exists in this sacrament, such as to live, to die, to grieve, to be animate or inanimate: whilst whatever belongs to him as regards outward bodies can be attributed to him, as he exists in his own species, but not as he is in the sacrament, such as to be mocked, spit upon, crucified. Hence the Versicle:

'Christ in the pyx, can grieve, and anguish feel,
But not the outward thorn, or nail or sharpened steel.'[1]

Obj. I. Christ's death was due to the Passion. But even then he would have been in the sacrament in an impassible way. Therefore he could not die in it.

Reply. Suffering is due to an external agent. Therefore Christ cannot suffer as he is in this sacrament, yet he can die [because death is due to the separation of body and soul].

Obj. II. At Christ's death his body and blood were separated. But they are together in this sacrament. Therefore Christ could not die in it.

Reply. Had this sacrament been consecrated when Christ died, his blood would have been really separated from his body; and the body only would have been under the species of bread, and the blood only under the species of the wine. Both are not really separated now; for by concomitance his blood is present with the body under the species of the bread and his body with the blood under the species of the wine.

Obj. III. Death is due to the separation of the soul and body. But both are in this sacrament. Therefore had it been reserved, Christ could not die in it.

---

[1] 'Pyxide servato poteris sociare dolorem,
Innatum: Sed non illatus convenit illi.'

Reply. Christ's soul is present by real concomitance, not by virtue of the consecration (cf. 76, 1); and when really separated at death from his body, it would not have been under this sacrament because of a different disposition of the thing itself, but not from any defect in the power of the words.

Chapter X

THE MINISTER OF THIS SACRAMENT

Does the Consecration of this Sacrament belong to a Priest alone? (Q. 82, 1)

Yes. This sacrament is of such dignity that it is effected only in the person of Christ. Whoever acts in the place of another must do so by the authority that person bestows. Now since the power of receiving this sacrament is bestowed by Christ on the baptized, so the power of consecrating this sacrament in the person of Christ is conferred on the priest at his ordination. For thereby he is put in the same plane as those to whom the Lord said: '*Do this for a commemoration of me*' (Luke 22, 19).

Hence St Isidore says: 'It belongs to a priest to perfect this sacrament of the Lord's body and blood upon God's altar.' Only a priest, therefore, can consummate this sacrament.

Obj. I. This sacrament is effected by the words of consecration; now these words are not changed whether spoken by a priest or anyone else. Therefore it seems anyone can consecrate.

Reply. The sacramental virtue of the Blessed Eucharist consists not in one element only, but in several; just as the sacramental virtue of Baptism consists neither in the words alone, nor in the water alone, but in both as united by the intention of him who baptizes. So, to consecrate validly, a man needs the priestly power imparted to him at his ordination, when the ordaining Bishop says to him:

'*Receive power of offering sacrifice in the Church as well for the living as for the dead.*'

Obj. II. But St Chrysostom says: 'Every holy man is a priest.'

Reply. A devout layman has a *spiritual*, but not a *sacramental* priesthood. Being united to Christ by faith, hope and charity, he can fruitfully offer to God spiritual victims and sacrifices. For a *sacrifice to God is an afflicted spirit;* and again, '*Present your bodies a living sacrifice*' (Rom. 12, 1). Hence St Peter says: '*A holy priesthood is to offer spiritual sacrifices.*' But this is quite a different thing from the sacrificial power of the official priesthood.

Obj. III. As Baptism is ordained for men's salvation, so also is this sacrament as said above (74, 1; 79, 2). Therefore it is not proper to a priest alone to consecrate since a layman can baptize.

Reply. The reception of the Eucharist is not of such necessity as that of Baptism, and therefore in urgent cases a layman can baptize but not consecrate.

Obj. IV. The consecration of holy oils belongs to a bishop, yet it is not of such dignity as the consecration of the Eucharist, which contains the whole Christ. Therefore only a bishop should consummate this sacrament.

Reply. The bishop receives power to act in the person of Christ upon his Mystical Body—the Church: whatever does not pertain to it is not reserved to the Bishop, such as the consecration of this sacrament.

But it belongs to the bishop to deliver not only to the people, but also to the priests whatever is needed to fulfil their respective duties. Hence the blessing of the holy oils, vestments, consecration of the altar and sacred vessels, are reserved to the bishop as the head of the whole ecclesiastical order.

Can several Priests Consecrate one and the same Host?
(Q. 82, 2)

Yes. According to the custom of certain churches, newly ordained priests celebrate together with the ordaining bishop. As just said, a priest by ordination stands on a level with those who received the power of consecrating at the Supper; and just as the apostles dined when Christ dined:[1] so the newly ordained can celebrate with the ordaining bishop. Nor is the consecration (successively) repeated over the same host because as Innocent III says: 'The intention of all should be directed to the same instant of consecration.'

Obj. I. Several cannot baptize together one person. Therefore several priests cannot consecrate one host at the same time.

Reply. Christ is not said to have baptized with the apostles when he imposed on them the duty of baptizing; therefore, here again there is no parity in these two sacraments.

Obj. II. Nothing ought to be superfluous in the sacraments. When one suffices to consecrate, how can several consecrate the one host?

Reply. If a priest were acting by his own power, any more than one celebrant would be superfluous. But since a priest consecrates only in the person of Christ; and since *many* are *one* in Christ, it makes no difference whether one or many consecrate except that the rite of the Church must be observed.

Obj. III. Multitude is apparently opposed to unity: How then can *many* priests consecrate the *same* host which becomes *the sacrament of unity* as St Augustine calls it?

Reply. The Eucharist is the sacrament of ecclesiastical

1 Our Lord *alone* consecrated at the Last Supper *in his own person*, but gave the power to consecrate to his apostles by the words: '*Do this for a commemoration of me*' (Luke 22, 19).

unity which is effected by *many being one in Christ*.
Does the distributing of this Sacrament belong to a priest alone?
(Q. 82, 3)

Yes. 'It has come to our knowledge that some priests
deliver the Lord's body to a layman or woman to carry to
the sick. The synod prohibits such presumption. The
priest himself shall communicate the sick.' (*De. Consecr.
Dist.* 12, Cap. 27).

The distributing of Christ's body belongs to the priest
for three reasons:

First. The priest consecrates in the person of Christ; and
as Christ consecrated his body at the Supper, so he himself gave it. Now since consecration belongs to the priest,
so also does the distributing.

Second. The priest is the intermediary between God
and the people; and as it is his duty to offer their gifts to
God, so it belongs to him to deliver consecrated gifts to
the people.

Third. Reverence for this sacrament demands that
nothing touches it but what is consecrated, for instance
the priest's hands, chalice and corporal; and it is not
lawful for anyone else to touch this sacrament unless
from necessity.

Obj. I. Distributing of this sacrament does not belong
to priests alone; for Christ's blood is given by deacons;
for instance, St Laurence said to St Sixtus: 'Try whether
you have chosen a suitable minister to whom you
have entrusted the dispensing of the Lord's blood.'

Reply. A deacon may dispense the blood,[1] but not the

---

[1] This custom is no longer observed.

According to Canon 845, a deacon may administer the Eucharist by leave
of the bishop or parish priest, provided there is a sufficient reason.

In case of necessity, permission may be presumed; but he cannot communicate himself if no other minister is present, except in case of great necessity,
whilst a priest may give Holy Communion to himself simply for the sake of
devotion.

body except in case of necessity at the command of a bishop or parish priest.

Obj. III. The Eucharist, like chrism, has the power of perfecting: but it belongs to bishops and not to priests to sign the baptized with chrism: therefore it also belongs to bishops and not to priests to dispense this sacrament.

Reply. Just as deacons share, in a way, in the priest's power of enlightening: so the priest himself shares in the bishop's power of perfecting the people and distributing this life-giving sacrament by which men are made perfect *personally* in relation to Christ. But other perfections by which a man is perfected in regard to his fellow-men are reserved to the bishop.

Is the Consecrating Priest bound to receive this Sacrament?
(Q. 82, 4)

Yes. '*As often as the sacrificing priest immolates the body and blood of our Lord on the altar he shall partake of that body and blood.*'

The Eucharist is not only a sacrament but also a sacrifice. Whoever offers sacrifice ought to share in it; because the exterior sacrifice is the sign of the interior sacrifice by which he offers himself to God.

Hence by partaking, he proves that the interior sacrifice is his also; and in the same way by distributing the sacrifice to the people, he shows that he is a distributor of divine gifts of which he himself should be the first to partake, as Dionysius says: 'Therefore the priest before distributing to the people ought to receive this sacrament in its integrity.'

Obj. II. No man can baptize himself. Therefore the priest who consecrates the Eucharist ought not to receive it at his own hands.

Reply. Baptism is perfected by the use of matter. So no one can baptize himself because in a sacrament the same person cannot be active and passive. Hence the priest does not consecrate himself, but he consecrates the bread and wine; and the use follows the sacrament.

Obj. III. Sometimes Christ's body miraculously appears on the altar under the form of flesh, and the blood under the guise of blood which are not suitable for food and drink. Hence as said above (75, 5) they are given under another species lest the communicants experience a feeling of horror.

Reply. If Christ's body appear under the form of flesh and his blood under the guise of blood, it is not to be received. For Origen[1] says: '*It is lawful to eat of this Host which is wonderfully sacrificed in memory of Christ: but it is not lawful for anyone to eat that which Christ offered, just as he was on the Cross.*'

Nor does the priest transgress on that account because miracles are not subject to ordinary laws. Still it would be advisable for the priest to consecrate again and receive the Lord's body and blood, under the sacramental species.

Can a bad priest Consecrate the Eucharist? (Q. 82, 5)

Yes. St Augustine says: 'In the mystery of the Lord's body, what is wrought by a good priest is not greater; and what is wrought by a bad priest is not less; because it is not wrought by the merits of the consecrator, but by the Creator's word and by the power of the Holy Ghost.'

The priest consecrates this sacrament not by his own power but as minister of Christ in whose power he sacrifices.

If he happens to be wicked, he does not cease to be a minister of Christ; for our Lord had them good and bad.

---

1 *De Consecrat,* C. 76, Dis. 2. In Washbourne's edition, third volume, QQ. LX—LXXXIII, p. 419, of English *Summa*, this passage is attributed to St Jerome.

And hence he says: '*Who thinkest thou is a faithful and wise servant?*' and afterwards he adds: '*But if an evil servant shall say in his heart*', etc. (Matt. 24, 45).

Again St Paul says: '*Let a man so account of us as ministers of Christ*', and afterwards adds: '*I am not conscious myself of anything, yet I am not thereby justified*' (1. Cor. 4, 1).

He was certain that he was a minister of Christ but not that he was a just one. So a man can be Christ's minister whether he is just or not; and this belongs to the excellence of Christ, whom, as the true God, good and evil serve; since by his providence they are ordained for his glory. Hence it is clear that priests—just or unjust—can consecrate the Eucharist.

Obj. I. St Jerome says: 'Priests who administer the Eucharist and who distribute our Lord's blood . . . act impiously against Christ's law by imagining that it is a prayer which consecrates the Eucharist and not a good life.' Therefore a sinful priest cannot consecrate.

Reply. St Jerome here reproves the error of those who believe they worthily consecrate, even though they are sinners, because they happen to be priests.

Obj. II. St John Damascene says: 'By the coming of the Holy Ghost, the bread and wine are supernaturally changed into the body and blood of the Lord.' But Pope Gelasius asks: 'How will the heavenly Spirit be present, if invoked by a priest who is steeped in sin?'

Reply. What Gelasius means is evident from what he previously said, viz., 'This most holy rite claims for itself such reverence that no one dare approach except with a clean conscience.' Hence there is question here not of validity but only of lawfulness.

Obj. III. This sacrament is consecrated by the priest's blessing. But if he is a sinner, it is not efficacious, for the prophet says: '*I will curse your blessings*' (Mal. 2, 2).

Reply. When done with a bad intention the same action can be evil on the part of the servant and good on the part of the master, when it was good he intended. So the blessing of a sinful priest, who acts unworthily, deserves a curse and is rather an infamy or blasphemy and by no means a prayer. *Yet when pronounced in the person of Christ, it is holy and efficacious for sanctification.* Hence, it is said with deep significance: '*I will curse your blessings.*'

Is the Mass of a wicked priest of less value than the Mass of a good priest? (Q. 82, 6)

Yes. The decretals say: 'The worthier the priest, the sooner he is heard for whom he prays.'

In the Mass, there is the sacrifice, the principle element, and the prayers for the living and the dead.

As a sacrifice the Mass is of equal value whether said by a good or by a bad priest. For the same sacrifice is offered by both.

As regards the *prayers*, there are (*a*) those said by the priest with personal devotion, and (*b*) those said in the place of the whole Church by the priest in the Mass.

(*a*) The devotion of the priest makes the prayers efficacious: so the better the priest the more fruitful the Mass.

(*b*) But since the ministry of Christ remains even in sinful men, as said above (Art. 5), in this respect the prayer even of the sinful priest is fruitful not only in the Mass but also in the ecclesiastical offices in which he takes the place of the Church: although his private prayers may not be efficacious according to Prov. 28, 9: '*He that turneth his ears from hearing the law, his prayers shall be an abomination.*'

Obj. II. As Baptism is conferred by a minister through the power of Christ, who baptizes, so also is this sacrament consecrated in the person of Christ. But, as said above (64, 1 ad 2) Baptism is not better when conferred by a better priest. Therefore neither is the Mass better when said by a worthier priest.

Reply. There are no solemn prayers offered in Baptism for all the faithful as in the Mass. There is, however, a similarity as to the effect of the sacrament.

Obj. III. If the Mass of a better priest is better, we could not say that the Mass of a bad priest is bad; for St Augustine writes that: 'The malice of the minister cannot react upon the mysteries of Christ.'[1]

Reply. The private good in the Mass of a good priest is fruitful to others by the power of the Holy Ghost who communicates to each one the riches of Christ's members who are united in charity. But the private evil of one man cannot injure another unless by some kind of a consent (cf. August. *Contra Parmen*. Lib. II, C. 12).

Can heretic, schismatic and excommunicate priests Consecrate? (Q. 82, 7)

Yes. St Augustine says: 'Just as Baptism remains in them (i.e., heretics, etc.) intact: so also do their Orders.'

Some held that the heretics, schismatics and the excommunicated cannot consecrate. But they are deceived in this; for St Augustine says: 'It is one thing not to have at all, and another *to have*, but not in a right way: and in the same way it is one thing to give and another to bestow, but not rightly.'[2]

Hence those ordained within the Church have the power of consecrating the Eucharist rightly indeed. But if separated by heresy, schism, or excommunication, they use their power improperly. Whilst those ordained when separated from the Church have neither the power rightly, nor do they use it rightly. But still in *both* cases

1 *Contra Donat*. XII.
2 *Contra Parmen*. Lib., III. C. 13, 21. Ibid. Lib. II.

they have the power, as St Augustine says, and when they return to the unity of the Church, they are not re-ordained but are admitted in their Orders.

By the power of those Orders, such as are separated by heresy, etc., can indeed consecrate the Eucharist, in which Christ's true body and blood are contained; but they act wrongly and sin by doing so; and therefore do not receive the fruit of the sacrifice which is a spiritual sacrifice.

Obj. I. St Augustine says: 'There is no such thing as a true sacrifice outside the Church.'

Reply. By a true sacrifice here is meant a spiritual sacrifice; that is, with the *truth of its fruit*. But the sacrifices of heretics, etc. are true sacrifices with the *truth of the sacrament* (i.e., our Lord's body is truly present): hence the sinner receives his body sacramentally but not spiritually.

Obj. II. Innocent I says: 'Even if we do receive the Arian laity, under the pretext of repentance, it does not follow that their clergy have the dignity of priesthood. . . . For we only allow them to confer Baptism.'

Reply. Baptism alone is allowed to be administered by heretics, etc., since they can baptize in case of necessity. But they cannot *lawfully* consecrate or confer the other sacraments.

Obj. III. When a priest consecrates, he does so in the person of the whole Church. How then can heretics, etc., consecrate the Eucharist when cut off from the Church?

Reply. The priest recites the prayers at Mass in the place of the Church in whose unity he remains, but when consecrating he speaks in the person of Christ.

Therefore a priest cut off from the unity of the Church, consecrates; but because he is cut off, his prayers have no efficacy.

Can a degraded priest Consecrate this Sacrament? (Q. 82, 8)

Yes. St Augustine proves that apostates are not deprived of their Baptism, since it is not restored when they repent; and therefore it cannot be lost.

For the same reason, a degraded priest is not re-ordained if restored and consequently has never lost the power of consecrating which belongs to the character of the priestly order.

But every character is indelible, because it is given with a kind of consecration, as said above (Q. 63, 5). Hence St Augustine says: 'It is not lawful for Catholics to repeat either Baptism or Orders (*Contra. Parmen.* II).

Obj. I. He who gives can take away. But the ordaining bishop gives the priest power to consecrate. Therefore he can take it away (by degrading him).

Reply. The bishop does not give the priestly power as if coming from himself, but as God's Minister; and its effects cannot be taken away by man. For 'What God has joined let no man put asunder' (Matt. 19, 6). Therefore the Bishop cannot take away this power, just as the one who baptizes cannot take away the baptismal character.

Is it lawful to receive Holy Communion from excommunicate, heretical or sinful priests, or assist at their Mass?

(Q. 82, 9)

No. The Canon says: 'Let no man hear the Mass of a priest whom he knows without doubt to have a concubine'; and St Gregory says: 'A treacherous father sent an Arian bishop to his son to receive from his hand, sacrilegiously, the Sacred Communion: but he was a man, and devoted to God and rightly rebuked the Arian on his arrival.'

Although, as said above, priests, whether they be heretics, schismatics, excommunicates, or criminals, have the power of consecrating; they do not use it properly, and sin by using it, and whoever communicates with them in their sin shares in it.

Hence St John writes: 'For, *he that says to him "God speed you"* (i.e., to a heretic) *communicateth with his wicked works'* (2 Epist. ii). Consequently it is not lawful to receive Communion from them or to assist at their Mass.

There is a difference, however, among the above classes: the first three are debarred from exercising their power of consecrating by a sentence of the Church.

But as regards sinful priests, until such a sentence is pronounced, it is lawful to receive Communion from them or assist at their Mass.

For, as St Augustine says, when the apostle writes, *'With such a one, not so much as eat'* (1 Cor. 5, 11) he does not wish one man to be judged by another on mere suspicion or even by usurped extraordinary judgment, but rather by God's law according to the regulations of the Church, whether the sinner confesses of his own accord, or be accused and convicted.

Obj. I. But St Augustine also says: 'No one should avoid God's sacraments whether given by a good or by a wicked man' (*Cont. Petil.* III, 9).

Reply. We are not avoiding God's sacrament when we refuse to hear the Masses of such priests or to receive Communions, but rather we are venerating them. Hence a Host consecrated by such priests is to be adored and if reserved it can be consumed by a lawful priest. So we shun *what is the sin* of the unworthy ministers, *not* the *sacrament.*

' Is it lawful for a priest to refrain altogether from Consecrating the Eucharist? (Q. 82, 10)

No. St Ambrose says it is a grievous thing for us not to approach the table with a clean heart and pure hands but still more grievous if while fearing sin we do not also offer Sacrifice.

Some said that the priest can lawfully refrain altogether from consecrating unless bound by the care of souls to celebrate and administer Sacraments.

But this is unreasonable because everyone is bound to use the grace given to him when the opportunity arises according to St Paul: 'We exhort you that you receive not the grace of God in vain' (2 Cor. 6, 1).

But the opportunity of offering sacrifice is not only to be considered in regard to the faithful to whom the sacraments must be administered, but principally in regard to God to whom sacrifice is offered by consecrating.

Hence it is not lawful for a priest to cease celebrating altogether even though he has not the care of souls; but he seems bound to celebrate at least on the chief festivals, and especially on those days on which the faithful usually communicate; for it is said against some priests that 'they were despising the Temple and neglecting the sacrifices' (2 Machabees 4, 14).

Obj. I. A priest is not bound to administer the sacraments unless he has care of souls; and if he has no such care, neither should he be bound to consecrate the Eucharist.

Reply. The other sacraments are perfected by the use of the faithful. Therefore only one in charge of souls is bound to administer them. But this sacrament is perfected in the consecration of the Eucharist whereby a sacrifice is offered to God to which the priest is bound from the Order he received.

Obj. III. The priestly dignity is not lost by subsequent weakness. But it happens sometimes that those who are ordained contract defects which prevent them from celebrating, such as leprosy or epilepsy. It appears then that priests are not bound to celebrate.

Reply. Sickness or weakness does not deprive one

already ordained of his Orders but prevents him from exercising them if he lost his sight for instance, or his fingers or the use of speech.

Introduction to Q. 83

This introduction must inevitably break the rule: 'Make not the porch larger than the mansion.' For, nowhere perhaps in the whole *Summa* does St Thomas express greater depth in fewer words than when proving the Mass is a sacrifice and the same as Calvary. First, because the celebration of this mystery is a certain image of the Passion.

Secondly. Because we share in its effects.

One may well ask, if the Mass be simply an *image* of Calvary, how is it a real sacrifice? The answer is: Each of us is a representative image of our first parent; and just as every man coming into the world re-presents Adam to the end of time, so in every Mass that is offered, the Passion will be re-presented to the great accounting day; but in a more perfect way.

For no natural image contains or can contain what it actually represents.

We only represent Adam in so far as we are all of the same species. But we do not represent the *individual man*— Adam that far surpassed us all in vigour and intelligence even in the Fall.

On the other hand the Mass not only represents the whole Passion and death of Christ but *contains* it. That is—it *is* the sacrifice of the Cross.

The Mass then differs only accidentally from the Passion.

By accidental difference is meant something that does not affect the substance or species. A man in perfect health is specifically the *same* as when bleeding to death. However great the difference between the states might be it is only accidental. But should he die the *difference* becomes

K

specific because he ceases to be man. This is the difficulty some theologians have felt in trying to explain how Christ was a victim in the Mass and how the Mass is the same as Calvary.

They overlooked the great central fact that the victim in both sacrifices is divine and that the Passion was a sacrifice and not merely martyrdom because of his will to suffer and die.

Now although the body and soul of Christ were separated from one another, the divinity was not separated from either—and body and soul were only separated because the victim, being divine, willed that they should be. Now it is the same will, which, so to speak, eternizes every action of the Passion in the Mass and makes both the same sacrifice, only different in mode.

Hence the condition in which he exists as victim in the Mass was brought about principally by his own will to die on the Cross and instrumentally by those who were permitted to make him suffer, and above all by every moment he did suffer, just as bread is made suitable for eating by every moment the heat of the fire acts upon it. *The Mass therefore is a Complete Sacrifice and the same as Calvary.*

First, because the same victim with the self same will to die *once* is made present. That is to say, the will that assumed the dread of punishment, the loathing and sorrow for sin, that bowed the back to the scourge, the head to the thorns, the shoulders to the Cross, opened the hands to the nails, and separated body and soul on the Cross is re-presented in the Mass because the Mass re-presents Calvary according to St Paul (1 Cor. 11, 26): *'For as often as you shall eat this bread and drink this chalice you shall show forth the death of the Lord.'*

The will to die once without actual death is typified by

Abraham's oblation, when St Thomas says: 'Isaac signified Christ as far as he was offered in sacrifice' (2, 2, 85, 1 ad 2). By sacrifice he means something a man makes sacred (2, 2, 85, 3 ad 3). And according to Sylvius[1] it is made sacred when accompanied by some change in the victim.

In Abraham's sacrifice the change in the victim was the surrender of his will to live, and this change in disposition was proved and externated, when in his early prime, Isaac allowed his aged father to bind and place him upon an altar to be slain and burned. For Isaac was no mere boy when he carried up the mountain-side all the wood necessary to make a holocaust of a human body.

Second. The Mass is also a complete sacrifice by reason of the effects. St Thomas's second argument is: 'That by celebration of this sacrament we share in the fruits of the Passion.' That is to say, the Mass is a sacrifice because only such an action[2] could produce the same effects as the Cross. Hence as every new generation arises, it needs the fruits of the *one sacrifice* to be applied to it; and this is only possible through the Mass, which, therefore, is a sacrifice, for here St Thomas follows St Chrysostom who says, 'The celebration of the Mass avails as much as the death of Christ on the Cross.'

So, the same victim who prayed for his persecutors, pardoned the penitent thief and made the dead rise, now raises untold numbers of spiritually dead every time Mass is offered.

1 Sylvius—(French *Du Bois*), a Belgian, born 1581—made Douai famous by his lectures on the *Summa*. His reply to the Jansenist who tried to win over that University on the pretext of defending St Augustine was characteristic: 'Yours is a Dutch Augustine. Ours is the great Augustine of Africa; for his is the teaching of the Sovereign Pontiffs for whom we are prepared to combat to the last breath.' He died in the odour of sanctity, 1649.

2 Action was the ancient name for the whole Mass, and is now restricted to the Canon.

For the Council of Trent says: 'The Lord being appeased by this oblation bestows grace and the gift of penance and pardons crimes even the most enormous.' (Sess. 22, Cap. 2.)

It may be objected that it does not follow if two effects are alike their causes are alike; for instance water power, steam and electricity can produce the same effects. There is *no parity*. For just as we prove the soul is a spiritual substance from the fact that the acts which flow from it are simple and indivisible, so from what the Church teaches about the effects of the Mass we must infer it is a sacrifice, and the selfsame as Calvary.

It may be further objected that Baptism and Penance also remit enormous crimes and neither of these is a sacrifice. Baptism and Penance benefit only the recipient (cf. 79, 7). But the Mass benefits others as well, i.e., not only the living but also the dead. Hence our Lord said '. . . . which for you' (who receive the Eucharist) 'and for many (others) shall be shed for the remission of sins.'

Chapter XI

THE RITE OF THIS SACRAMENT

Is Christ Sacrificed in this Sacrament? (Q. 83, 1)

YES. St Augustine says: 'Christ was once immolated in himself and yet he is daily immolated in this sacrament.'

First. The same saint says: 'Images are called by the names of those things which they represent, as when we look on a picture or fresco we say, 'This is Cicero.' 'That is Sallust.' ''

Now the celebration of this sacrament is a certain representative image[1] of Christ's Passion which is his true immolation. Therefore the celebration of this sacrament is called the sacrifice of Christ.

Hence St Ambrose says: 'In Christ, was once offered a victim capable of giving eternal salvation. What then do we do? Do we not offer it up every day but in memory of his death?'

Second. In another way by reason of the *effects* of the Passion, this sacrament is called the sacrifice of Christ since by it we become partakers of the fruit of his sufferings.

Hence we say in the Mass: '*Wherever the commemoration of this Sacrifice is celebrated the work of our redemption is wrought.*'

Therefore in regard to the first way (in which Mass is a

---

1 St Thomas's words are: 'Celebratio hujus sacramenti imago quaedam est repraesentativa Passionis Christi quae est vera ejus immolatio.' See appendix for questions 'Is the Passion itself a true sacrifice?' and 'Is the immolation of the Mass *real* or simply mystical?'

sacrifice) Christ could be truly said to be sacrificed even in the figures of the Old Law. And hence St John speaks of '*The Lamb slain from the beginning of the world*' (Apoc. 13, 8).

Obj. I. How can Christ be offered and immolated again when it is written: '*Christ by one oblation hath perfected for ever them that are sanctified*' (Heb. 10, 14)?

Reply. St Ambrose says: 'There is but one victim (which Christ offered and which we offer) and not many, because Christ was offered but once.'

But the one sacrifice is the pattern of the other. For just as what is offered everywhere is one body and not many: so also is it but one sacrifice.

Obj. II. The immolation of Christ was made on the Cross whereon he delivered himself for us an oblation and a sacrifice to God (Eph. 5, 11). But Christ is not crucified in the celebration of this mystery.[1] Therefore neither is he sacrificed.

Reply. As the celebration of this sacrifice is an image representing Christ's Passion, so the altar is a representation of the Cross upon which Christ was sacrificed in his own species.

Obj. III. In Christ's sacrifice the priest and victim are one and the same. But in the Mass the priest and victim are not the same. Therefore it is not Christ's sacrifice.

Reply. For the same reason just given, the priest also bears the image of Christ in whose person and by whose

[1] Christ immolated himself on the Cross by allowing the Jews to crucify him; and in the Mass he also *really* immolates himself by representing that same will to die *once*. For it was this will that made the crucifixion a sacrifice, and not merely a martyrdom. Hence, St Gregory says: 'Christ inflicted on himself, what permitted wickedness devised' (Morals Job, II, 6). And it is the same will which makes him still priest and victim of the one *sacrifice*. (See appendix II, p. 174.)

In other words, Christ on the Cross annihilated space and time by making his sacred body present on countless altars, and his will to die once, to be renewed to the end of the world.

power he pronounces the words of consecration, as is clear from what was said above (82, 1 and 3). So in a way the priest and victim are one and the same.

Introduction to Article 2, Q. 83
Note on objection from St Augustine

St Augustine asks in this article: 'Is Christ not slain as often as the Pasch (i.e., the Mass) is celebrated?'

How is Christ said to be slain *when he dieth no more?* (Rom. 6, 5). In every sacrifice there are four elements:[1]

(1) The external sacrificial act of the offerer testifying to the interior sacrifice of the will and intellect.

(2) Some kind of change in the victim, physical or moral.

(3) Acceptance by God: '*The Lord smelled a sweet savour*' (cf. Gen. 8, 21).

(4) Sacrificial effects (ibid.) '*I will no more curse the earth.*'

(A) *In Abraham's sacrifice of Isaac there were:*

First. The sacrificial act: building altar, placing wood for holocaust, binding victim, raising the sword—all testifying to the interior sacrifice of the will and intellect.

Secondly, change in the victim: A moral change—having free will and power to enforce his choice, gives external proof of change of disposition by allowing himself to be bound and placed on an altar, thus surrendering his will to live.

Thirdly, acceptance by God as a sacrifice who said by his angel: '*Because thou hast not spared thy son*' (Gen. 22, 16).

Fourthly, effects: '*I will multiply thy seed*' (Ibid, 5, 16): that is, unity in multitude.

1 There are also four things necessary for every sacrifice:
    (1) Sacrificial gift.
    (2) Sacrificing minister.
    (3) Sacrificial action.
    (4) Sacrificial end or object.

(B) *In the Last Supper and in the Mass (by his minister)*:

First. Sacrificial act: Christ raised his eyes, gave thanks, blessed, broke, sacrificial words, distributed (cf. Maldonatus: Luke 24, 30).

Secondly. Change in victim: from his own proper species to his sacramental species; proving his will to die once by giving his body and blood in a sacrificial condition, suitable for eating and drinking to the end of time, and all as a result of his death on the Cross.

Hence he is said to be slain.

Thirdly. Acceptance by God: his body and blood are ever united to the divinity by concomitance in that sacrificial state; and even though his soul and body were separated on the Cross, still his divinity would remain united to each and each be infinitely acceptable.

Fourthly. Effects: unity founded on humility and mutual love (cf. Luke 22, 27; John 14, 23).

'That they all may be one as thou father in me and I in thee, that they all may be one in us' (John 17, 21).

Has the time for celebrating this Mystery been properly determined? (Q. 83, 2)

Yes. By the custom observed by the Church and according to Canonical Statutes.

The time suitable for celebrating the mysteries is determined by what they represent, viz., the Passion, and by its fruits in which we participate. As we daily need these fruits owing to our daily defects, this sacrament is offered daily.

Hence our Lord teaches us to entreat: 'Give us this day our daily bread' (Luke 11, 3). And St Augustine asks: 'If it be daily bread, why do you take it but once a year as the Greeks do in the East? Receive it daily that it may benefit thee daily.'

Obj. I. This sacrament is commemorated but once a

year. For St Augustine says: 'Is Christ not slain as often as the Pasch is celebrated?' But yet the yearly remembrance represents what happened long ago and so causes[1] us to be moved, as if we saw our Lord hanging on the Cross. Therefore this sacrament should be celebrated only once a year.

Reply. Christ's Passion is commemorated in this sacrament in two ways:

First. According as it was accomplished *once* in our Head: the Passion is therefore fitly commemorated in Lenten time.

Secondly. According as the fruits actually reach the faithful who receive them daily: the Passion is commemorated every day for the sake of these fruits and to provide a perpetual memorial.

Obj. II. It seems unfitting to celebrate three times on Christmas Day this sacrifice which commemorates the Passion and omit it entirely on Good Friday.

Reply. In our Mass and Blessed Sacrament there are two separate aspects (*a*) the Mass is in the first place itself a real sacrifice; (*b*) it is also a commemorative representation of the great sacrifice wrought on Calvary. Hence, on Good Friday when we gather in spirit once more on Calvary and gaze directly at the great oblation we feel the commemorative representation somewhat out of place;[2]

---

1 This is according to Marietti's Edition: 'Et sic nos facit movere.' The English Dominican translation reads: 'And so it *does not* cause us to be stirred, etc.'

2 This reply is a paraphrase: St Thomas answers that the Mass is a figure or pattern of the Passion, and therefore this sacrament is not consecrated on the day in which the Passion is recalled, as it was really accomplished.

'Figure' is derived from 'fingere' to mould.

In the Mass as on Calvary, Christ is the High Priest, or Offerer, and Victim. It was the Cross that moulded, so to speak, the Victim of the altar (cf. 81, 3, Obj. I), and only in that sense can the Mass be called a figure of the Passion, for the same *Reality* is the Victim in both sacrifices, bloody and unbloody, and present in the latter as St Thomas says (83, 3), '*Not in figure, but in very truth.*' p. 151.

so neither host nor chalice is consecrated on that day. But lest the Church be on that day without the fruit of the Passion offered to us in this sacrament, the body of Christ is consecrated the day before and reserved to be consumed on Good Friday.

On Christmas Day, however, several Masses are said on account of Christ's threefold birth. The first is his eternal birth hidden from us and therefore one Mass is said in the night; and in the introit we say 'The Lord said to me, thou art my Son. This day have I begotten thee.'

The second is his nativity in time and the spiritual birth whereby Christ rises as the day star in our hearts (2 Pet. 1, 19). And therefore the Mass is sung at dawn; and in the introit we say 'The light shall shine on us today.'

The third is his temporal and bodily birth when coming forth from the Virgin's womb and being clothed with flesh, he became visible to us. So the Mass is said in the clear daylight; and in the introit we say: 'A child is born to us.'

Still on the other hand, his eternal generation can be said to be in broad daylight; and therefore in the third Mass the eternal birth is mentioned.

As regards his corporal nativity, literally he was born at night as a sign that he came in the darkness of our infirmity. Hence at the midnight Mass the Gospel of Christ's Corporal Nativity is said.

Obj. III. Christ consecrated this sacrament in the evening, therefore it ought to be celebrated in the evening.

Reply. As said already (73, 5) Christ wished to give this sacrament last to impress it more deeply on the hearts of the disciples; and therefore consecrated it after supper at the close of the day.

But we celebrate at the hour our Lord suffered, either on festivals at the hour of Terce when he was crucified by the tongues[1] of the Jews and when the Holy Ghost[2] descended on the disciples, or in ferias at the hour of Sext when he was crucified by the soldiers,[3] or on fast days at None when crying with a loud voice he gave up the ghost.[4]

(Now according to Canon 821, Mass is to be said not sooner than an hour before dawn nor later than an hour after midday.)

Ought this Sacrament be celebrated in a house with Sacred Vessels? (Q. 83, 3)

Whatever Christ ordains, the Church ordains: for 'wherever two or three are gathered together in my name there am I in the midst of them.'

Of the things touching upon this sacrament, two are to be considered:

First: What belongs to the representation of the Passion.

Secondly: What pertains to the reverence due to him, who is present not in figure but in very truth.

It is obvious then that whatever is used in the sacrament should be consecrated to show respect and to represent the effect of holiness derived from the Passion according to the Hebrews 13, 12:

'*Jesus that he might sanctify the people by his own blood suffered without the gate.*'

Obj. I. When Christ suffered outside the city gate and not in a house, this sacrament ought to be celebrated in the open.

Reply. Not as a rule. Its celebration should be in a house whereby the Church is signified according to I Timothy 3, 15: '*That thou mayest know how thou oughtest to behave thyself in the house of God which is the Church of the living*

---

1 Mark 15, 25.　　　　2 Acts 2, 15.
3 John 19, 14.　　　　4 Matthew 27, 46.

God.' Now as the Church was not to be confined to Jewish territory but was to be established the world over, therefore the Passion was not consummated in Jerusalem itself but out in the open that the whole world might serve as a house for Christ's Passion.

However, the book on Consecration says: 'We permit travellers to celebrate Mass in the open or in a tent if there is no church available, provided they have a consecrated table, and whatever else the sacred mysteries require.'

Obj. II. The house in which Christ consummated this sacrament was not consecrated, but merely an ordinary supper room prepared by the master of the house. Again we read in the Acts (2, 46) 'The apostles were breaking bread from house to house.' There is no need therefore for the house to be consecrated, in which the sacrament is celebrated.

Reply. St Thomas answers at length, but not directly:

The house, he says, wherein the sacrament is celebrated denotes the church, and is called one. So, it is fittingly consecrated to represent the holiness acquired by the Church through the Passion, and to typify the sanctity required by those who have to receive this sacrament. The altar signifies Christ himself; and its consecration his sanctity, of which St Luke says: '*The holy one born of thee*' (1, 35). And because Christ's sanctity is the source of all the Church's holiness, a consecrated altar suffices for consummating this sacrament in case of necessity.

Therefore a church is never consecrated without consecrating an altar. But an altar is often consecrated apart from a church, and along with it the relics of saints, '*whose lives are hidden with Christ in God*' (Col. 3, 3).

Obj. III. Nothing should be done in vain in the Church governed by the Holy Spirit. But it seems useless to consecrate a church or an altar since they are incapable of receiving grace or spiritual virtue.

Reply. Consecration does give them a special spiritual virtue in this way, that man derives devotion therefrom . . . unless prevented by want of reverence.

Hence the Scriptures say: 'There is undoubtedly in that place a certain power of God. For he that hath his dwelling in the heavens, is the visitor of and protector of that place' (2 Mac. 3, 38).

Therefore some say with probability that venial sin is forgiven by entering a consecrated church (just as it is by sprinkling holy water) as a result of the virtue acquired by the consecration.

The consecration is never repeated unless it is doubtful, or the church itself is destroyed by fire or defiled by the shedding of blood or by lust.

Secondly. The altar coverings, chairs, chalices, candlesticks, and veils are not to be used except in another church; otherwise they are to be burned.

Obj. IV. Only divine works should be solemnly commemorated according to the words of the Psalm 91, 5. 'I shall rejoice in the works of thy hands.' But the church or altar is consecrated by the intermediary of man just as a chalice or priest is. But the consecration of a chalice or priest is not solemnly commemorated, therefore neither should that of a church or altar be commemorated.

Reply. Consecration of the altar denotes Christ's sanctity, and that of the building, the holiness of the entire church. Therefore it is becoming to commemorate its consecration for the space of eight days to signify the happy rising of Christ and of the members of the Church.

Obj. V. In the Old Testament, the figure of the New, altars were not to be made of hewn stone, but stone which iron did not touch, or of earth or of setim wood (Exod.

20, 24, 25). Why then should the Church now use altars exclusively made of (carved) stone?

Reply. The command to make the altar of earth or of unhewn stone was to prevent idolatry.

Obj. VI. The chalice and paten represent Christ's tomb which was hewn in a rock. So they should be of stone, not of gold or silver or of tin.

Reply. Formerly the priests used wooden,[1] not golden chalices. Then Pope Zephyrinus ordered the paten to be made of glass; and later Pope Urban commanded all to be made of silver.

Afterwards, on account of the reverence due to this sacrament, it was enacted that the chalice and paten were either to be entirely of gold, silver, or tin, but not of brass or copper on account of the danger of verdigris. No one was to presume to sing Mass with a wooden or glass chalice. For wood being porous the consecrated blood would remain; and glass was fragile as also was stone.

Obj. VII. Chalices are made of gold because it is so precious. Therefore the altar cloths should be of silk because it is more valuable than linen.

Reply. The Church uses whatever more expressively represents Christ's Passion, where there is no danger. For this reason the chalice is not made of stone; but the corporal is made of linen, since Christ's body was wrapped in it; and linen owing to its cleanliness denotes purity of conscience, and also Christ's Passion on account of the labour spent on its preparation.

Obj. VIII. Christ's words must suffice for consecration; consequently the above-mentioned regulations seem unfitting.

---

1 St Bernard was very hard on the priests of his day when he said: 'Of old their hearts were of gold and their chalices of wood: now their chalices are of gold and their hearts are of wood.'

Reply. Dispensing the sacraments belongs to the ministers of the Church (and they can make regulations regarding it). But as the consecration is from God himself they can make no rules about the form of consecration or the manner of celebrating. Therefore if the priest pronounces the words over the proper matter with the intention of consecrating without house, altar, consecrated chalice, and corporal or whatever else is instituted by the Church, he sins gravely in not observing its rite; but still he consecrates Christ's body in very truth.

Have the words used throughout the Mass been fitly chosen?
(Q. 83, 4)

Yes. St Thomas's authority for this affirmative was the Book of Consecration which stated that it was James the brother of the Lord and Basil of Caesarea who edited the rite of saying Mass.

The authors of this book probably mean the Liturgy of St James, formerly used in Jerusalem and still followed by the Jacobites and Syrian uniates.[1]

The Rite of the Mass as we have it was evolved in the Catacombs. Even in Rome, Mass was said in Greek during the first century; and as it ceased to be spoken by the educated classes, Latin took its place.

The earliest sources of the present Roman Liturgy were the Leonine, Gelasian, and Gregorian sacramentaries. To these we owe the present fixed form of words and ceremonies which differ from the Eastern Liturgies by a practical sobriety in rubrics and clearness, conciseness and solidity of doctrine.

So what St Thomas says of St James and St Basil may apply to the early Popes. Obviously their authority guarantees the suitableness of every word. And as this sacrament comprises the whole mystery of our salvation,

1 Cf. Callewaert, *Liturgical Institutions*, T.I.

it is celebrated with greater solemnity than the rest.

But since it is written: 'Before prayer, prepare thy soul', the celebration of this mystery is preceded by a certain preparation to enable us to perform worthily what follows:

First. The first part is divine praise and consists in the introit: '*For the sacrifice of praise shall glorify me*, and there is the way by which I will show him the salvation of God' (Ps. 39, 23). Praise for the most part is taken from the psalms or at least sung with some of them, because Dionysius says: 'The Psalms comprise by way of praise whatever is written in the Scriptures.'

Second. In the second part we pray for mercy owing to our present misery, saying 'Kyrie Eleison' ('Lord have pity on us') three times for the person of the Father: 'Christe Eleison' ('Christ have pity on us') thrice for the person of the Son, and again 'Kyrie Eleison' three times for the person of the Holy Ghost, against the triple misery of ignorance, sin and punishment or else to signify *circumincession* or the existence in each other of the three Divine Persons.

Third. The third part commemorates heavenly glory to which we tend after this life of misery, by saying: 'Glory be to God on high.'

Fourth. The fourth part is the priest's prayer that the people may be worthy of such great mysteries.

Fifth. Next, as becomes this mystery of faith (cf. 78, 3 ad 5), is the instruction of the faithful, given *dispositively* in the Epistle when the teaching of the prophets and apostles is read aloud.

Sixth. Then the choir sings the Gradual signifying progress in life, and afterwards the Alleluia denoting spiritual joy, or else the Tract or spiritual groaning in mournful offices.

Seventh. But as the people are instructed perfectly by Christ's teaching in the Gospel; and because we believe he is the Divine Truth, the Creed is sung, and by it the people prove their assent by faith to his doctrine: for he said himself: 'If I tell you the truth, why do you not believe in me?' (John 8, 46).

Eighth. After the preparation and instruction of the people comes the celebration of the mystery. Now since it is *offered* as a *sacrifice* and *consecrated* and received as a sacrament, we have:

(*a*) The Oblation.

(*b*) The consecration of the matter offered.

(*c*) Its Reception.

Ninth. As regards the Oblation, first comes the Offertory, or the praise of the people expressing the joy of the offerers, and secondly, the priest's prayer begging God to accept the people's oblation.

Hence David said, '*In the simplicity of my heart I have offered these things; and I have seen with great joy, the people offer their offerings*' (1 Par. 29, 17).

Tenth. Since the consecration is due to supernatural power, the people are then admonished in the Preface to lift up their hearts to God, so as to excite their devotion. And when it is ended, they praise Christ's divinity by saying with the angels, 'Holy, Holy, Holy', and his humanity by saying with the children: 'Blessed is he that cometh in the name of the Lord.'

Next the priest secretly commemorates all for whom the sacrifice is offered, viz., the whole Church, those in high places (1 Tim. 2, 2) and particularly those who offer, or for whom the Mass is offered.

Then he invokes the saints to protect those he has just commemorated and says: 'Communicating with, and venerating first and foremost the glorious and ever Virgin,

L

etc.'. And lastly thus concludes: 'Therefore . . . this offering we pray thee accept that it may be salutary to those for whom it is offered.'[1]

Then comes the consecration, and first the priest asks for its effect: 'Which offering do thou O God deign to hold blessed . . . that it may become for us the body and blood of thy most beloved Son.'

Next he says the words (denoting a sacrificial act): 'Who, the day before he suffered, took bread', etc., and he effects the consecration by our Saviour's own words: 'This is my body', 'This is the chalice of my blood.'

Thirdly, he excuses his presumption by saying he obeys Christ's command: 'Wherefore being mindful of the blessed Passion.'

Fourthly, he asks the sacrifice now accomplished to be accepted by God: 'Deign to look with a propitious countenance.'

Finally, he begs for the effect of this sacrifice and sacrament. First, for the partakers: 'Suppliantly we ask thee that all of us, who, by participation in this altar, have received the body and blood of thy Son . . . may be filled to the full with every grace and benediction.'

Secondly, he prays for the dead who cannot receive it: 'Be mindful too, O Lord, of thy servants who have gone before us with the sign of faith, and sleep the sleep of peace.'

Next is the prayer for the priest himself who offers: 'And to us sinners, yet thy servants, whose hope is in the multitude of thy mercies.'

Now comes the preparation for reception of this sacrament:

1 St Thomas's words: 'Ut haec oblatio sit illis pro quibus offertur salutaris', are not found in modern missals.

First, the people are prepared to receive it by the prayer common to all, viz., the Lord's Prayer, in which we ask for our daily bread; and also by the private prayer: 'Deliver us from all evils, past, present and to come' offered specially by the priest for the people, who are again prepared by the peace given when the Agnus Dei is said: 'For this is the sacrament of peace and unity' (cf. 78, 4; 79, 1).

But as the Requiem Masses are offered not for present peace, but for the repose of the faithful departed, in them the Pax is omitted.

Then comes the reception; and as Dionysius says: 'He who gives divine things to others ought first to be a partaker himself', so the priest receives before he gives to anyone else.

The Mass ends with the thanksgiving on the part of the priest and with rejoicing on the part of the people for having partaken of this mystery. Hence the singing after Communion and the priest's prayer of thanks, as Christ after the supper said a hymn (Matt. 27, 30).

Obj. II. Words and actions occur at the consecration not given in the Gospels. For instance, we do not read of Christ lifting up his eyes, or using the word *All* when saying, '*Take ye and eat.*'

Reply. St John writes that Christ said and did many things not mentioned by the Evangelists. Among these is the raising of his eyes to heaven at the Last Supper which the apostles handed down to the Roman Church: 'He lifted up his eyes to his Father when raising Lazarus' (John 11, 41); and when praying for his disciples (ibid., 18, 1). He had greater reason to do so when instituting this sacrament.

The word *All* is understood in the Gospel although not expressed. For he said: '*Except you eat the flesh of the Son of Man . . . you shall not have life in you'* (John 6, 54).

Obj. III. All the sacraments are ordained for our salvation. But there are no common prayers in their celebration for either the salvation of all the faithful or of the departed. So it is unbecoming in this sacrament.

Reply. The Eucharist is the sacrament of unity of the whole Church, therefore mention ought to be made in it more than all the other sacraments of all that belongs to the salvation of the whole Church.

Obj. VI. Every word spoken in this sacrament should be said by the priest since he is the minister.

Reply. As just said, what belongs to the whole Church is mentioned in this sacrament. So the choir sings what refers to the people. But there are other words which the priest begins and the people continue, to show that they signify what has come to the people through divine revelation, such as faith and glory. Therefore the priest intones the Creed and Gloria and says aloud whatever words are common to priests and people. But what belongs to the priest alone, such as the oblation and consecration, he says in secret.

In both, however, he arouses the people's attention by saying 'Dominus vobiscum'; and waits for their reply: 'And with thy spirit' ('Et cum spiritu tuo') signifying their assent.

Obj. VII. Divine power works infallibly in this sacrament. There is no necessity then for the priest to say: 'Which oblation do thou O God deign to hold blessed, approved, ratified, and acceptable, that it may become for us the body and blood of thy most beloved Son.'

Reply. The priest's intention can impede the efficacy of the sacramental words. It is not unbecoming to ask God for what he will do, just as Christ did for his glorification (John 17, 1, 5). Yet the priest does not seem to pray for the fulfilment of the consecration but rather that it may be fruitful in us. Hence, he says expressly: 'That it may become for us the body and blood of Christ': again the preceding words bear out this meaning: 'Deign to hold *blessed*', i.e., according to St Augustine, 'That we may receive a blessing, i.e., through grace: *Approved*, i.e., that we may be incorporated in the bowels of Christ: *Reasonable*, i.e., that we who are displeasing to ourselves may through it become pleasing to his Son (*Paschas. De Corp. et Sang. Dom.* XII).

Obj. IX. Just as Christ's body does not begin to be in this sacrament by change of place (cf. 75, 2), so neither does it cease to be there by change of place. Therefore the priest should not say: 'Bid this be carried up by the hands of thy holy angels to thine altar on high.'

Reply. This does not refer to Christ's true body, but to his mystical body signified in this sacrament and means that the angel present at the divine mystery may present to God the prayers of both priest and people according to the Apocalypse: '*The smoke of the incense of the prayers of the saints ascended up before God, from the hand of the angel*' (8, 4).

The altar on high means either the Church triumphant to which we beg to be transferred, or God himself, whose participation we pray for (i.e., to share in the divine nature). Or again by the angel is meant Christ himself, who is the Angel of great council (Isaias ix, 4). (For we must bear in mind that the word 'Angel' means 'One sent'.) And he unites his mystical body with God the Father and the Church Triumphant, and hence the Mass derives its name (*Missa*) because the priest sends (*mittit*) his prayers to God through the Angel, as the people do through the priest. Or else because Christ is the Victim sent (*Missa*) to us by God. So on Festival days the

deacon says: 'Ite missa est'; that is, the Victim has been
sent (*missa est*) to God through the Angel, so that it may
be accepted by him.

The actions that are done in the celebration of the Mass, that is,
various rites and ceremonies included in it, have they been aptly
chosen? (Q. 83, 5)

To make their inner meaning clearer the sacraments
have a twofold signification in words and actions (cf. Q.
60, 5 and 6).

Now this sacrament represents Christ's Passion,
signifies his mystical body, and demands great reverence.
Consequently, some things are done in its celebration
which belong to devotion and respect, and others to
represent Christ's Passion or the disposing of his mystical
body.

Obj. I. Washing the hands was one of the ceremonies of
the Old Law which are not to be observed under the New
Testament. Therefore it is not becoming for a priest to
wash his hands when saying Mass.

Reply. The Church observes the ceremony not because
the Old Law did so, but because it is becoming in itself.
For we do not handle precious objects unless the hands are
washed. Again, as Dionysius says, 'The washing of the
extremities signifies the cleansing from the smallest sins.'
Another reason is that the hand is the *organ of organs*
(*De Anima* VI) and all works are attributed to it. Hence
David says: '*I will wash my hands among the innocent*'
(Ps. 25, 6).

Obj. III. Actions performed in this sacrament ought
not to be repeated. The priest therefore should not make
the sign of the Cross so often over it.

Reply. The sign of the Cross signifies the Passion that
ended on the Cross itself, and was accomplished in certain
stages:

First. The betrayal due to God,[1] the Jews, and Judas is signified by the triple sign of the Cross at the words 'Haec dona, haec munera, haec sancta sacrificia illibata' ('These gifts, these presents, these holy unspotted sacrifices').

Secondly. The selling of Christ to the priests, the Scribes and the Pharisees is signified by the threefold Cross at the words 'Benedictam, adscriptam, ratam' ('Blessed, enrolled, ratified'). Or again to show that he was sold for thirty pence, and a double Cross is added at the words: 'That it may become the body and blood of thy most beloved Son' to signify the person of Judas, the seller, and of Christ, who was sold.

Thirdly. To denote the foreshadowing of the Passion at the Last Supper, two crosses are made, each while saying, 'He blesses' at the consecration of the body and at that of the blood.

Fourthly. We come to the Passion itself; and to represent the five sacred wounds there is a five-fold signing of the Cross at the words, 'Hostiam puram, hostiam sanctam, hostiam immaculatam, panem sanctum vitae aeternae, et calicem salutis perpetuae.'

Fifthly. The stretching of the body and shedding of the blood and the fruit of the Passion are represented by the triple signing of the Cross at the words 'Corpus et Sanguinem sumpserimus' ('as many as shall receive the body and blood may be filled with every blessing').

Sixthly. Christ's threefold prayer on the Cross is represented by a triple signing of the Cross at the words 'Sanctificas, vivificas, benedicis'; the first for his persecutors: 'Father, forgive them'; the second for deliverance from death, and the third regarding his approaching glorification. 'Father, into thy hands I commend my spirit.'

Seventhly. The triple sign of the Cross at the words

---

1 Because he willed it; see appendix II, p. 174.

'Per ipsum et cum ipso et in ipso' ('Through him, and with him and in him') representing the three hours he hung upon the Cross.

Eighthly. The separation of his soul and body is signified by the two subsequent crosses made outside the chalice.

Ninthly. The Resurrection on the third day is represented by the three crosses at the words 'Pax domini sit semper vobiscum' ('May the peace of the Lord be ever with you').

Briefly, it may be said that the consecration and acceptance of this sacrament and its fruits proceed from the virtue of the Cross of Christ and therefore the priest uses the sign of the Cross when any of them is mentioned.

Obj. V. It seems absurd for the priest to stretch out his arms, join his hands or close his fingers, etc.

Reply. These gestures are not absurd when done to represent something else.

The arms extended signify Christ's outstretched arms upon the Cross. The hands uplifted show that prayer is being directed to God for the people, according to Lament. 3, 41, '*Let us lift up our hearts with our hands to the Lord in the heavens*', and again '*When Moses lifted up his hands Israel overcame*' (Exodus 17, 11).

When the priest joins his hands and bows, he denotes the humility and obedience of Christ, as a result of which he suffered. The fingers are closed out of reverence after the consecration: because they touch the consecrated body of Christ; and lest any particle adhering to the fingers might be lost.

Obj. VI. It seems ridiculous for the priest to turn round to the people and greet them. Such things ought, therefore, not to be done during the celebration of this sacrament.

Reply. The priest turns five times to the people to

signify that our Lord manifested himself five times on the day of his Resurrection (cf. III, 45, 3). And again the priest salutes the people seven times to denote the sevenfold grace of the Holy Spirit—five times when turning round to the people and twice without turning, when he says at the Preface 'The Lord be with you' and again 'May the peace of the Lord be ever with you' before the Agnus Dei.

Obj. VII. Christ ought not to be divided. But he is in this sacrament after the consecration.

Reply. The breaking of the Host does not suppose any division of Christ; but denotes, first, the division of his body during the Passion. Secondly, the distinction of his mystical body according to the different states. Thirdly, the distribution of graces that flow from Christ's Passion.

Obj. VIII. But the body of Christ was divided during the Passion in the places of the five wounds. Therefore the same body in this sacrament ought to be broken into five parts instead of three.

Reply. Pope Sergius says: 'The Lord's body is three-fold: the part offered and put into the chalice shows that Christ's body is now risen. Namely, Christ himself and the Blessed Virgin, and if there are any other saints in glory at present with their bodies. The part consumed represents those still walking on earth; because they are united whilst here by this sacrament and are bruised by the passions, just as bread when eaten is bruised by the teeth. The part reserved on the altar until the close of the Mass is his body lying in the sepulchre because the bodies of the saints will be in their graves until the end of the world, though their souls are either in Purgatory or in Heaven. However, this rite of reserving to the end of Mass one part is no longer observed on account of the danger, but the same meaning of the parts still holds.

Can the Church's Statutes sufficiently meet the defects during this Sacrament? (Q. 83, 6)

Yes. Just as God does not command impossibilities so neither does the Church. Dangers or defects that may occur are met in two ways: First, by prevention. Second, by rectifying whatever is wrong, either by applying a remedy or by doing penance in case of neglect.

Hence: (1) If a priest dies, or becomes seriously ill before the consecration of our Lord's body and blood, there is no need to complete it. But if after the consecration is begun or even completed, some other priest must finish the Mass. 'For as we are all one in Christ, the change of persons does no harm where unity of faith effects a happy consummation' (Council of Toledo).

(2) When a difficulty arises, follow the least dangerous course. The greatest danger in this sacrament arises if it is not completed; for this is a horrible sacrilege, but the danger is much less as regards the receiver.

Consequently a priest remembering after the consecration that he has eaten or drunk, ought to complete the sacrifice and receive. Or again if he remembers he is in sin, he should make an act of contrition with the intention of confessing and making satisfaction, and thus will not unworthily but fruitfully receive.

The same holds if he remembers he is excommunicated, for he should resolve humbly[1] to seek absolution and so he will obtain absolution from the Invisible High Priest Jesus Christ, for his act of completing the divine mysteries.

(3) If a fly or spider fall into the chalice before consecration, or if the wine is found to be poisoned, it must be poured out, the chalice purified and fresh wine put in.

---

[1] We can infer from this how easy it is to make an act of perfect contrition according to St Thomas.

But if after the consecration, the insect should be thoroughly washed, then burned and the ashes put into the sacrarium. Or if the wine is poisoned, it is to be kept in a suitable vessel, and other wine put into the chalice and the Mass resumed, from the consecration of the blood.

(4) If after the words of consecration the priest finds there is no wine in the chalice (a) before receiving the body, he must put in fresh wine with the water and repeat the words of consecration of the blood; (b) if after receiving the body, he finds no wine in the chalice, he should get another host and consecrate it along with the blood and receive both, even if he already has taken water which was in the chalice, because the precept of completing this sacrament is more important than that of receiving it fasting, as said (80, 8).

(5) A priest who does not recollect saying some of the words he should have said, ought not to be disturbed; for a man who speaks many words cannot remember them all, unless he adverted to something in connection with what was said.

If it is probable that the priest has omitted some words not necessary for the sacrament, I do not think he should repeat them, changing the order of the sacrifice, but ought to continue.

If, however, he is certain that he did omit any of the words necessary for the consecration of the sacrament, he should do what was said above (4): repeat the form of consecration and all that is necessary to be done so that the order of the sacrifice be not changed.

.   .   .   .   .

This is the last question St Thomas wrote on the sacrament he loved. He discussed seven more on the sacrament of penance and laid down his pen. His lifework was done.

At the Council of Trent his *Summa* held the place of honour next to the Sacred Scriptures. He lived there again in his writings and still lives and shall until time is no more.

The fathers at that council summed up all he said here on the sacrifice of the altar in these words which cannot be too often repeated, or too often reduced to practice whenever possible:

NO OTHER WORK SO HOLY AND DIVINE CAN BE ENGAGED IN BY THE CHRISTIAN FAITHFUL AS THIS SAME TREMENDOUS MYSTERY.

LAUS DEO SEMPER ET MARIÆ.

APPENDIX I

SAINT THOMAS calls the Passion our Lord's true immolation (83, 1). Is this immolation a sacrifice, or in other words:

Was the Passion itself a complete sacrifice?

In *The Mystery of Human Faith and Opinion Contrasted and Defined*, by Père De La Taille, s.j. (Sheed and Ward, 1930) we read the following: 'As regards immolation . . . the Passion sufficiently accounts for it. But the Passion was the work of the executioners and not of Jesus. It cannot therefore by itself alone constitute a ritual oblation. . . . Where shall we find this oblation which is absolutely indispensable, if the death of Jesus is to be a sacrifice properly so called, and not a sacrifice in the broad sense, a purely metaphorical sacrifice such as martyrdom under the New or under the Old Law.

'From the Garden to the Cross this oblation appears nowhere in spite of the efforts of some to locate it in this or that stage of the bloody drama, efforts which, moreover, do not bear analysis' (p. 10).

These lines seem to have been written without reflection; for the Passion was nothing else but a ritual oblation from beginning to end.

It was to atone for the Fall. The Fall was due to pride and love of pleasure. So every detail was thought out before the Passion came to pass; and many of them explicitly set forth in the Scriptures; and all were deliberately designed to humiliate and torture.

What more suitable altar for sacrifice than that which was never mentioned in polite society in Athens, Rome,

Carthage in their hey-day, and was held in execration by the Jews—the limit of torment and disgrace—*the cross?*

In this twentieth century when the Cross is honoured everywhere, we cannot realize the words of St Paul: 'We preach Christ crucified, unto the Jews *indeed* a stumbling block and unto the Gentiles foolishness' (1 Cor. 1, 23).

The idea of the Creator dying the death of a criminal was unthinkable. So it was to prepare us and convince that such a series of unspeakable sufferings and degradation were set forth in detail as the *Ritus Servandus* of the Passion, by the prophets and by our Lord himself.

But when asking: 'Where do we see the sacrificing mind?' Father De La Taille seemed to imply that if the Passion was to be a ritual oblation without the Last Supper, our Lord should have been clothed in some peculiar way to impress on us the fact that he was offering himself as a victim with solemn rites.

So he was. But he did not will to wear those sacerdotal garments that inspire profound respect.

No. The only liturgical vestments he wore when offering his bloody sacrifice were those which excited derision and contempt—the white garment of the fool, and the tawdry purple of the mock king.

At the very moment he sustains all things, the Infinite Wisdom arrayed in these is the sport of Herod's courtiers and Pilate's soldiers.

That is to say, being offerer as well as victim, he wore the liturgical vestments suitable to a sacrifice of degradation and yet of triumphal expiation: and when divested not only of these but of his own, his very nakedness was part of the rubrics he willed to observe, according to the *Ritus Servandus* set forth in the 21st Psalm: 'They divided my garments amongst them.' Father De La

Taille or many another far less gifted might point to a St Peter, a St Andrew or a St Laurence and say that they too were stripped naked and tortured, but still the surrender of their lives was simply a metaphorical sacrifice and that so would the Passion have been, only for the ritual oblation of the Last Supper. Moreover were the sufferings of St Peter, St Andrew and St Laurence not due to the executioners and so also the Passion? For we have just heard that 'It, too, was the work of the executioners, not of Jesus.'

The test proving the Passion of itself is a divine and true sacrifice, and not simply martyrdom, is the answer to the following questions:

(1) Do martyrs arrange all the details of how they are to suffer and die?

(2) Suppose we restrict the word 'Passion' to suffering alone inflicted by the executioners: was it they who caused the blood to flow from every pore in the garden? Or did they make him cry out on the Cross the prophetical words of David: '*My God, my God, why hast thou forsaken me?*'

(3) Have any of the martyrs deliberately breathed forth their spirit? Or, in other words, was any single death of theirs due to an act of their own will and yet not a felo de se?

(4) Have any of them ever cried out with a loud voice when absolutely exhausted and on the point of expiring in such a way as to make bystanders exclaim: '*This is the Son of God*'?

(5) Could any of them at that moment prove their dominion over death by opening the tombs; or when any of them died, was the whole world covered with darkness?

(6) If the Passion was all the work of the executioners

how were they able to eclipse the sun; and why did Amos prophesy that event? (8, 9).

Save when the earth quaked and the veil of the temple was rent, the eclipse was the most awe-inspiring ceremony of the bloody sacrifice; and yet it was more wonderful in its setting.

For although St Matthew tells us that 'There was darkness all over the world from the sixth to the ninth hour', the priests blinded by jealousy, that same passion that brought about the Fall, taunted their Victim with the very same words that they sang with a show of reverence in the temple: '*He hath hoped in the Lord, let him take him and save him*' (Ps. 27, 7).

This, they thought was an unanswerable challenge to throw down or rather *up* to him—and all the while they were carrying out ceremonies allotted to them as *victimarii*, or rather as demons.

For they meant to prove to the world that his miracles were counterfeit and that he himself was an impostor.

Every sacrifice was accompanied by prayer (cf. Allies. *Form. of Christd. B.V.*, pp. 241-250).

The one prayer that soared above the massed chorus of blasphemies of priests, people and soldiers was 'Father, forgive them' (Luke 23, 34).

By that prayer he saved those blasphemers from the fate of Core at the very moment they were taunting their Creator for not saving himself.

Not only did our Lord refuse to take up their challenge, but as priest and victim he carried out the most humiliating and degrading of all ceremonies and sufferings, hanging on in agony and verifying the words of Isaias: 'With the wicked he was reputed', and thus willed to be regarded as an impostor by those of whom the same Isaias prophesied: 'Their eyes they have shut lest they should see.'

For at the same moment he bowed his head on the Cross those in the temple watched the veil being rent, not from the bottom up, but from the top down, that is, in the same direction as he bowed his head, and they must have soon heard that at the same moment the dead arose and yet they went to Pilate after all this for a guard to watch the tomb.

A rite is defined as a formal act of religion, observance, ordinance. When were more formal acts of religion carried out and ordinances observed than from Gethsemane to Golgotha when he exclaimed: 'It is consummated'?

Appendix II

IS THERE A REAL IMMOLATION IN
THE MASS?

Saint Thomas says (Q. 83, 2 ad 2): 'When the reality
appears the figure ceases. Therefore on the day on which
the Passion is recalled as it was really accomplished this
sacrament is not celebrated.'

Some theologians infer from these words that there is
only a mystical but not a real *immolation* in the Mass.

They forget that what really occurred on Good Friday
was all foreseen, arranged and permitted—and *willed* at
every stage and it was the will of Christ that immolated
him, not the executioners.

Hence St Thomas says (III, 47, 4): 'The Passion of
Christ was an offering of sacrifice in so far as Christ by
his own will endured it from pure charity. But in so
far as he suffered from his persecutors it was not a sacrifice but a most grave sin.'

Again (in Q. 48, 3 ad 3) he says: 'The Passion of Christ
on the part of the executioners was a malefice—but on the
part of Christ suffering from charity was a sacrifice.'

The word 'Immolation' is derived from 'Mola' or
salted barley meal which was sprinkled by the priest on
the head of the victim, and does not necessarily mean the
actual suffering or slaying of the victim.

This (the killing) was done in most cases, not by the
priest, but by one called the *popa* or *victimarius* who
felled the victim, and the priest carried the blood to the
altar.

Our Lord immolated himself somewhat after this manner when he went into the very place where he was to be apprehended, and fell on his face and suffered a deadly fear, sadness, and loathing of sin to seize upon him, and thus cause his blood to flow.

But immolation could not mean that he should offer himself in sacrifice by laying violent hands on himself. But it meant that he did not hinder the Jews from doing so, when he could have prevented them.

'Immolation', says Father Brosnan (*Sacrifice of the New Law*, p. 61), 'is the action of the priest which makes the victim of the outward sacrifice.'

According to Father Swaby, O.P., St Thomas teaches (83, 1) that 'The bloody sacrifice, the *true* immolation is identical with the Passion (from Garden to Cross).' Thus St Thomas says: 'The Passion of Christ which is his true immolation' (*The Last Supper and Calvary*, p. 80).

Now as our redemption was directly effected by the death on the Cross—every act of our Lord from Gethsemane was deliberately intended to bring about that all-merciful consummation: in this sense he sacrificed himself at every moment from the time he entered the Garden till he bowed his head on the Cross.

For instance he immolated himself—that is—he made himself the victim of the outward sacrifice, by allowing himself to be bound and dragged before Annas and Caiphas to be judged by the very men who had already condemned him to death.

This sacrificial act was absolutely voluntary even at the moment when surrounded and with no apparent escape; for when our Lord asked his captors: '*Whom do you seek?*', not even Judas knew him. (cf. St Chrysostom 83, Hom. St John.)

There was immolation in every word and no blood-shedding when he said: 'This is your hour and the power of darkness' (Luke 22, 53). 'If you seek me, let these go their way' (John 18, 8).

He was giving the word of command, and only when it was obeyed did he suffer himself to be bound and led away.

Again he immolated himself by his silence before Herod and Pilate when a word could have saved him.

He was the lamb before the shearer who opened not his mouth, but he could not let Pilate's arrogance go unchallenged when Pilate said: 'I have power to crucify thee and I have power to release thee.' For immediately he reminded him that he had no power save what was given from above (John 19, 10, 11).

And even when he did allow Pilate to deliver him up to be crucified, all the might of Rome could not deprive him of life; and he did what no other could do: he surrendered his own life by simply breathing forth his soul at the moment he chose himself.

This was the supreme act of immolation and yet even in death he willed that his side should be pierced and that water and blood should flow from it.

St Augustine and St Chrysostom agree that from the wounded heart the Sacred Mysteries derive their origin (cf. a Lapide, John 19, 33).

Hence we have in both sacrifices the same *will* that forbade *a bone to be broken*, separated the body from the soul and united them in the tomb and placed them on the altar with the self-same virtues exercised in every moment as in the Passion.

For these reasons St Thomas calls the Mass the 'Exemplum Dominicae Passionis' or the archetype of the Lord's sufferings; and since the same victim is present on the altar as he was in every stage in the Passion there must be a *real* immolation otherwise there is no real victim present and the Mass is not a representation of Calvary.

If it be urged, how can our Lord be a real victim in the *Mass* when he no longer suffers or dies? it must be remembered that the Mass is only a sacrifice because it represents sufferings *once* endured and death *once* undergone, and applies the fruits (83, 1).

When St Thomas therefore speaks of the Mass not being celebrated on the day on which the Passion is recalled as it was really accomplished he meant those actual sufferings and the actual humiliation to which the victim was once subjected.

Appendix III

MAN'S FALL AND EXALTATION

Saint Thomas gives an objection from St Chrysostom, 'Every holy man is a priest', and replies 'a devout layman has a spiritual but not a sacramental priesthood' (III, 82, 1).

But the priest turns to the people and says: '*Pray, brethren, that your sacrifice and mine be acceptable to God, the Father Almighty.*'

(1) These words remind the faithful that they are not mere spectators but that they share in the fruits as well as the priest himself. Hence in the early Church it was the rule that *all* should receive a part of what was consecrated and not merely the priest himself (III, 80, 10).

(2) Again the faithful could say it was their sacrifice when at the offering their oblations were placed on the altar to be *converted* into the body and blood of Christ (III, 77, 6).

(3) Yet in another sense, by virtue of the sacramental character received at Baptism, the faithful offer sacrifice through their priest, of adoration, praise, thanks, petition, propitiation, and this is the privilege of man, beyond all other creatures God ever made (III, 73, 3; and 80, 9 ad 3.).

Hence St Peter calls the faithful a holy priesthood who offer spiritual sacrifices—a chosen generation, a kingly priesthood; and we have a striking proof of this in the first chapter of Genesis: because of Abel's sacrifice he became its first martyr, so to speak. 'Then God gave another seed for Abel called Seth; and to Seth was born

Enos who began to call upon the name of the Lord'
(Gen. 4, 25, 26). Only the names and ages of Seth's
descendants are given, and when God sent the Deluge, the
only family to survive was the ninth in the direct line; and
when Noah came out of the Ark, his first act was to build
an altar and taking of *all* cattle and fowls that were clean,
offered holocausts. And the Lord smelt a sweet savour
(signifying his acceptance) and said 'I will no more curse
the earth for the sake of man' (Gen. 8, 20, 21).

But God is love and God is charity. Why did he
permit sin to so abound that he was forced to curse the
earth and bring on the Deluge? When Adam fell, murder
followed disobedience, then lust and selfishness, so much
so that God repented that he made man.

He did not make him without knowing too well what
was going to happen. Could he not have created Adam
with the perfect obedience of Abraham, and Eve with
the absolute sinlessness of Mary?

God never intended man to suffer. The danger of
sinning was reduced to a minimum. Only one tree out of
thousands was forbidden, to test man if he really loved
his creator; for our Lord says: 'If you love me, keep my
commandments.'

The test proved that man merely loved himself and
would aspire to be his own maker; and like the Pharisees
in the temple, thank himself for all his gifts of nature and
grace, and ask nothing.

The Fall opened his eyes. When he was in honour he
did not understand; now he realized his absolute depend-
ence on his Maker, and being humbled he became grateful
and felt all the more the need of asking him for his daily
wants, and pardon for his daily sins.

Thus by the fact of sin and suffering being permitted,
man became the most perfect sacrificial being in God's

creation. For as his nature was wounded by sin he keenly felt the necessity of turning to his Creator. Thus the idea of sacrifice became an instinct, and when the Creator himself assumed our human nature, and came in the likeness of sinful flesh (Roms. 8, 3) and offered it on the Cross, and when he renews that sacrifice in the Mass through the intermediary of man, man is raised above the angels and surpasses all other creatures, as the mouthpiece of creation in adoring, praising and thanking his Creator.

Appendix IV

By D.Ph.

Mathematical Quantity. Discussing the objects of the various sciences St Thomas says, after Aristotle (*Metap. Lib.* IV, lect. i, and *Lib.* VI, lect. i) that the object of the *physical* sciences is gained by *a first degree of abstraction* whereby the individuating notes are left aside and we consider *universal sensible matter.* By a second degree of abstraction all qualitative aspects are left aside so that we consider only *intelligible matter.* This is *mathematical quantity*, the object of the science of mathematics. Such an object does not include sensible matter in its meaning but is quantity *considered apart from all sensible matter and its qualities.* Hence mathematical quantity is quantity considered as purely intelligible; it is simply magnitude, whether continuous (geometry) or discontinuous (arithmetic, etc.).

Dimensive Quantity, on the other hand is more general and does not imply that one considers purely the intelligible aspect abstracting from sensible matter. On this see I Q. 77, Art. 2 ad 4um.

Materia signata: On this question I will try to avoid as far as possible all discussion or justification of St Thomas's opinion on the principle of individuation, though something must be said of it to explain the passages referred to in the *Summa* or even to explain the term 'signata': regarding this principle of individuation St Thomas says: 'Materia non quomodolibet accepta principium est individuationis, sed solum materia signata.' He then

173

explains the term: 'Et dico materiam signatam, quae sub certis dimensionibus consideratur.' (*De Ente et Essentia*, 2 par. cf. I Sent. d. 25, Q. 1 ad 2). The word *sub* is important. Materia signata is opposed to materia universalis seu communis. 'Haec autem materia (signata) in definitione hominis, in quantum homo, non ponitur, sed poneretur in definitione Socratis, si Socrates definitionem haberet; in definitione autem hominis ponitur materia non signata; non autem in definitione hominis ponitur hoc os et haec caro, sed os et caro absolute, quae sunt materiae non signatae.' Later St Thomas changed his opinion on this principle under the influence of Averroes and in *IV Sent.* and more clearly in *In Boethium De Trin.* Q. 4, a 2, maintains that the principle is 'materia signata quae dimensionibus *indeterminatis* subest.' He later left this opinion so we need not consider the meaning of signata in such an interpretation. (cf. *C. Gentes*, c. 63, 65, and *de Subst. separis*, c. 5.)

Now these 'certis dimensionibus' spoken of above come to matter by means of the substantial form of corporiety and are ontologically consequent on it. An accident cannot be the principle of substantial individuation; accidents[1] are secondary acts and are consequent on the union of Matter and Form; they are determined and individuated by the substance in which they inhere (cf. I. Q. 76, Art. 6, and also 4 *De Spirit. Creat.*, A. 3; *De anima*, A. 9). Yet St Thomas seems to say that these quantitative determined dimensions individuate matter or make it signate; besides there is the common formula representing his doctrine by 'materia quantitate signata'. Then in the article with which the query deals St Thomas

---

1 Accidents alone cannot be a principle of individuation, which is to be found in the nature of the substance itself; and as this nature has within it a relationship to the basic accident of quantity, it provides the principle.

speaks of *quantitas dimensiva* as '*Quoddam individuationis principium*' (III, Q. 77, A. 2). The explanation as I see it is this: Just as *materia prima* is the first subject of the substantial form, so dimensive quantity (not mathematical but physical quantity) is, in the accidental order, the first subject of the other accidents for they all inhere in substance *mediante quantitate*. Hence the accidents are individuated proximately and immediately *mediante quantitate* so that the quantity can be called 'quoddam principium individuationis'—it is the principle of individuation in the accidental order. But that has not settled the question of *materia signata* or *materia signata quantitate* for the accidental principle of individuation presupposes an ultimate and fundamental one in the substantial order which is the real *materia signata*. On this point there are several opinions even amongst Thomists (1) Sylvester Ferrariensis (In lum., Gent. c. 21) claims that it is matter which is determined by *actual quantity*, i.e., quantity (an accident) is the condition of the individuality of the substance in so far as it is by reason of quantity that a substance is subject to determinations in space and time. This opinion, for the reasons above of accidents, seems quite unacceptable.

(2) Cajetan and John of St Thomas hold that *materia* is *signata* by a capacity or receptive potency for this special quantity rather than any other; it is *materia sub certis dimensionibus and not cum certis*, etc. To understand this it must be remembered that matter and form are *co-principles* one for the other so that though materia signata is the fundamental principle it *is not the whole principle* for the co-principle is made specially for it. 'Materia prima recipit formam, non prout est forma simpliciter, sed prout "est hoc".' (II *Sent*. A. 3, Q. 1, A.1 ad 3.)

There are a few precisions which should be made regarding the development of St Thomas's thought whereby he built up the doctrine of '*de ente et essentia*', and made it more precise as he saw the consequences; but it is sufficiently accurate as it stands.

Appendix V

NOTES

ACCIDENTS, SUBSTANCE AND DIMENSIVE QUANTITY

INTRODUCTION. Page xi. When accidents are said to inhere in dimensive quantity, dimensive quantity is only the immediate subject which itself inheres in a substance, therefore ultimately all accidents inhere in a substance apart from the miracle of the Blessed Sacrament.

Page xii. Substance is independent of all accidents in so far as it need not have this determined quantity or quality rather than any other, but when it is corporeal it must have some quantity and is not independent in that sense. The trouble in philosophy is that a simple statement is often a half truth and a half truth masquerading as a whole truth is an error.

Page 21. Q. 75, Art. 4. Technically and strictly speaking the word *change* is associated with *natural changes*, i.e., where something remains and something passes. But of course it stands if dissociated from and opposed to natural changes whether substantial or accidental. St Thomas makes *conversio* much wider than *mutatio* and uses only the former of transubstantiation.

Literal Translation of third reason given by St Thomas (77, 2), p. 51.

Since the subject is the principle of individuation of the accidents, then what is regarded as the subject of some accidents must be in the same way the principle of individuation: for the very name of an individual implies that it cannot be in many.

This happens in two ways:

First. Because it is not natural for an individual *to be in something else*. Thus immaterial separated forms subsisting of themselves are also individuals of themselves.

Secondly. Because any form—substantial or accidental is naturally in some one thing, not in several, for instance *this* whiteness in this *body*.

As to the first, matter is the principle of individuation for all inherent forms, because since such forms . . . are naturally in something as in a subject, then when any form is receives in matter and not in something else—it cannot whilst there, be in any other.

As to the second: the principle of individuation is dimensive quantity.

That one thing is naturally alone in another thing is because that other thing is undivided in itself and distinct from all others. Substance is divided by reason of quantity. Therefore dimensive quantity itself is a particular principle of individuation since forms numerically distinct are in different parts of matter. Hence dimensive quantity has also of itself a kind of individuation, so that we can imagine several lines (lineas) of the same species differing in position which (dimensive) quantity implies, for it belongs to dimensions to be *quantity having position* and therefore dimensive quantity can be the subject of the accidents rather than the other way about.[1]

---

[1] See page 48 concerning 'Dimensive Quantity', to which this note refers.